THE PSYCHOLOGY OF THE 12 STEPS

AN EXPERIENTIAL AND ACADEMIC JOURNEY THROUGH AA'S PROCESS OF RECOVERY.

PAUL V.Z. PSY. D.

authorHOUSE

AuthorHouse™
1663 Liberty Drive
Bloomington, IN 47403
www.authorhouse.com
Phone: 833-262-8899

© 2021 Paul V.Z. Psy. D. All rights reserved.

No part of this book may be reproduced, stored in a retrieval system, or transmitted by any means without the written permission of the author.

Published by AuthorHouse 04/13/2021

ISBN: 978-1-6655-1611-2 (sc)
ISBN: 978-1-6655-1610-5 (hc)
ISBN: 978-1-6655-1609-9 (e)

Library of Congress Control Number: 2021902485

Print information available on the last page.

Any people depicted in stock imagery provided by Getty Images are models, and such images are being used for illustrative purposes only. Certain stock imagery © Getty Images.

This book is printed on acid-free paper.

Because of the dynamic nature of the Internet, any web addresses or links contained in this book may have changed since publication and may no longer be valid. The views expressed in this work are solely those of the author and do not necessarily reflect the views of the publisher, and the publisher hereby disclaims any responsibility for them.

For questions, concerns or inquiries, Please contact me at; pvzlmft@gmail.com

Contents

My Story 1

Treatment Centers and Alcoholics Anonymous 15

The Psychodynamic Perspective 44

Adlerian Psychotherapy 57

Existentialism 74

Humanistic Psychologies 91

Behavioralism 98

Cognitive Behavioral Theory/Therapy 106

Al-Anon, Adult Children of Alcoholics,
and Emotions Anonymous 116

Conclusion 127

References 131

My Story

Hello. My name is Paul, and I am an alcoholic.

Hello. My name is Paul, and I am a psychologist.

I can confidently state that the latter would not be possible without the 12 steps of Alcoholics Anonymous. However, it is not as simple as that. The steps of the program are only a part of the entire experience. "The fellowship" which many a crusty "old timer" (member with a lot of sober time) will emphasize is *not the program,* was also a large part of my recovery from alcohol and drug addiction.

This work is an attempt to aid in the understanding of how the 12-step programs work and can be implemented in treatment. Or at the very least, outline the homogenization between 12-step principles and the theoretical and therapeutic aspects of psychology and psychotherapy. The fields of medicine and psychiatry, as well as psychology, which dominate the current treatment industry, in my experience and opinion, can, should and could be facilitating more productive outcomes with the people whom they treat. Specifically, I am speaking of maintaining long term sobriety and implementing the skills for living a satisfying life in said people. Also, I believe it is important to include the many lessons I and others have learned, as members of these 12 Step societies which were important in achieving and maintaining sobriety.

A primary motivation for my seeking an advanced degree in

psychology was the belief that my experience of getting sober could serve as a crucial element in my work as a psychotherapist. Also, I thought it would be an effective avenue in the fight against alcohol and drug addiction while possibly making the world a little bit better place for all to live. For the most part, I believe the aforementioned modalities *want* to make a difference in the fight, however the clinics that I have worked in, which focus on medicine and psychology first are missing the proverbial boat. As far as the medical fraternity is concerned, I do not understand the logic in trying to cure a substance abuser by giving them more substances, but that is not my scope of practice. Notwithstanding, these ideas will be covered in more detail in later chapters from an informed perspective.

As is the custom in A.A. and in some schools of psychological thought, I will start with an abridged version of my story. I am a first generation American of a Dutch father and a Burmese (called Myanmar today) mother. I am what is known by some as an Eurasian American, though this ethnicity cannot be found on today's cultural heritage questionnaires. I was raised in a suburban middle-class environment and have two siblings who are significantly older than I am. I am an Adlerian double whammy, if you will, as I am the youngest and because of the age difference, somewhat of an only child.

From what I can tell from the elementary school report cards my mother saved, I was a fairly well-behaved child; at first. At the point that my parents separated, coupled with ensuing chaos, I saw my "citizenship," also known as my behavior grades suffer. This phenomenon is in concordance with research findings in family systems psychology. Consequently, I do not think I would have noticed this without my training as a therapist. This started in about the fifth grade and continued throughout high school, culminating in my expulsion from the entire school district. I attended and completed my high school education in an independent study program which seemed a better fit for me. I achieved good grades while making up the semester that I was behind in order to graduate on schedule.

I never viewed myself, at least consciously, as a dropout or flunky. I also never viewed myself as intelligent either. I remember that my sister brought me a Preppy Handbook when she came back from college in New York. The icon that resonated with me was "the good old boy." One descriptor was "a genetically attached beer can to hand." This event occurred was when I was entering junior high school. I had already begun drinking occasionally whenever possible at that age. The good old boy became my identity throughout high school, and I tried to hold true to form. The mistaken belief that it was my God given right, as a red blooded American to be drunk most, if not all the time is what sustained the delusion that I was a normal drinker throughout my adult years. At times I would surrender to the idea that I was an alcoholic. However, the problem was that I believed an Alcoholic/Addict could stop or control their drinking and drug use if they wanted to. I did not understand what it meant to be an alcoholic. Other thought distortions which were maintained by drinking and drugging included the idea that people who were not homeless, were not alcoholics. Additionally,

I would argue that the fact I did not use certain drugs confirmed I did not have a drug problem. Of course, none of this was true.

Manipulation, whether it be that of one's self or that of another is a talent of many who are chemically dependent and mentally ill. My parents instilled the belief that I needed to find a way to survive in society. This loosely translated into… "Get a job!" I was working in the restaurant industry as a food server during high school and needed a solution for both my desire to be drunk and high as much as possible, with the need for a career. So, I arrived at the conclusion that I would become a gourmet chef. From what I had seen working in kitchens, that seemed like the solution to the problem. As I was attempting to complete my high school education in said independent study program, I was able to start working full time. I started my first cook job.

This was better than I imagined, as the ritual on shift break included a drive down the block to grab a couple of cold ones. We would return from break with "supplies" to be hidden in a back-storage room to finish the day. After work this would continue well into the evening and started all over again the next day. My next job was at one of the more prestigious hotel chains in the area. Given the propensity for manipulation which seemed a part of my alcoholic character, I was able to posture myself by using my talent, as what appeared to be a promising addition. I found that I was simply "casing" out the place if you will. Really what I was doing was seeking and setting myself up for the easiest and safest access to drink. Much to my joy, not long into my tenure, following the completion of a large banquet's food service, the executive chef appeared with a case of Heineken's. Almost needless to say, this provided me the green light to stay almost insanely drunk for nearly the duration of my employment there. There was a strange kind of codependence in the kitchen workers at that establishment, as well as throughout the industry then, which eventually seemed to only reinforce the importance of skill over drunkenness. What is more, it seemed as if the idea of partying was what most of my colleagues were interested in. Afternoon shift starts, leading to late nights of what began as fun was just what the doctor ordered for this alcoholic.

Undoubtedly, I became interested in making this a career choice. What alcoholic would not have? After a short time, it became evident that getting more training may be in order, if I was serious about making a true go at becoming a chef. Of course, because of an inflated sense of self, or possibly an overcompensation for a lack of one, I did not want to just become a chef. I wanted to become the next Wolfgang Puck, who was prominent at the time. So, I started to take classes at the local community college in preparation for the eventual transfer to the Culinary Institute of America in Hyde Park, NY. The school was the holy grail of culinary education, with several the world's top chefs having attended and graduated from that program.

The school is in what was considered upstate NY but is only something like a 90-minute train ride from NYC. The terrain was forest like and very rural compared to what I was used to growing up. This environment coupled with the various personalities attending made this experience interesting at the very least. I found myself amongst like-minded peers especially where the subject of drinking and drugging was concerned. I had several close calls as far as expulsion went, but again for reasons I cannot explain... I skated by. Was it my skill and ability in the kitchen? I do not know. Upon completion of my training, I was offered a job in the restaurant of a man whose signature was on my degree. However, in a sentimental, drunken and distorted frame of mind; I declined. I was likely filled with fear/anxiety as well, but those feelings were covered up by the alcohol and drugs. Though it could be just as likely that I did not even notice the significance of his name because I was consistently in a state of inebriation. The realization of who the man was that made me that offer only came sometime after returning home. Could this realization have created more distress which I tried to cover up with more alcohol and other psychological distortions? Probably.

A constant cycle of starting new jobs, fighting with management then quitting began to become common in my career as a professional chef. I did not know if my defiance was part of my alcoholism or possibly related to the internal strife which manifests in people with psychological issues. I did not know if my anger was also a part of that dynamic or if I only thought I was supposed to be angry. I was able to twist my mistaken beliefs in a way that I honestly believed I *deserved* to be drunk all the time. I did not understand the concept of working my way up through the ranks, but thought I deserved a promotion to the chef's position based solely on having graduated from *that* culinary school. This is where that Adlerian double whammy really comes into play and was expressed in the entitled behavior of the pampered child (an Adlerian concept). I had an attitude that shouted, "Don't you know who I am," when essentially all I was a potential; an action waiting to fire.

The decision or choice was mine. Which road would I choose? Subsequently, I chose the alcoholic journey and the eventual pain it would cause myself and those who cared about me. But did I really choose? Or even have a choice for that matter? This brings up a point of contention as the idea of an alcoholic/addict ability to choose to drink or use is a debate between professionals and the 12-step societies. Of course, this is not a literal debate in which both sides actively engage. It is a metaphorical one which, in my opinion is crucial to the propagation of long-term sobriety in individuals. The idea of choice where drink and drugs are concerned will be discussed and expanded upon in a further chapter.

So, my life continued this way for many years following my graduation from culinary school. I think it must have been my *potential* which provided me with so many close calls. Early on, it was true that I was not experiencing negative consequences for my actions. Well, not negative in the sense that I considered changing my modem operando. Nonetheless, a pattern of work and social relationships developed which illustrated the title… *short duration*. I had never been fired from a job up to this point, but I walked out of many as a result of my "don't you know who I am" mentality. After being fired for the first time, I began to wonder if maybe I or better yet, my drinking had something to do with it. This may have been the first point of contention which prompted a touch of insight, as related to the possibility I may be an alcoholic. Oddly, the two driving under the influence charges I received (in less than a month) shortly following completion of chef's school were chalked up to bad luck rather than the possibility I was an alcoholic. The largely denial driven assessment of bad luck was easier to negotiate psychologically than the possibility of a life without alcohol and weed (and other drugs). This was especially true in the future I had envisioned for myself. I told myself that "I had just graduated from the best culinary school in the world and nothing could stop me."

Eventually, this cycle of failed work and personal relationships continued long enough for me to start getting tired of it. Also, I was highly dissatisfied with the way my life was going. It was not playing out in the way I had planned it. I decided to prove to myself that I did not have a problem. I decided that I would quit drinking and smoking pot (and other drugs) for a year. During that period, I found myself re-engaging in physical activities I had neglected for the party lifestyle I imagined I was living. I also began to read inspirational books, attend church and meditate regularly. Coincidentally, around this time my father purchased tickets for myself and my siblings to attend a Zig Ziglar sponsored motivational seminar. My siblings purchased a set of tapes, but somehow, I ended up with them. I did not just listen to those Zig Ziglar tapes, I studied and engaged in the program as he laid out. I switched addictions in a manner of speaking. Though it was more like switching obsessions. Yet, one was obviously more productive than the other.

As a result of Zig Ziglar's program, I was transformed into a conscientious employee, arriving on time for work daily with a pleasant attitude. The restaurant I was working at was in one of the more renowned golfing resorts in the area. It was also known for winning many top honors in the area. The chef was a fellow alumnus, who was a colleague of the first chef whom I worked with upon graduation. Within a period of a few months, I was promoted to my first chef's position at one of the other golf resorts the company owned. This property was home to a PGA certified golf course and commanded such attention. I was the restaurant's Chef de Cuisine. I was given free range to create the entire menu and the required recipes. It was a dream come true. My personal relationships were also improving and providing me with much satisfaction in my life. I finally felt like I had arrived and become a success.

For whatever reason, a lack of insight possibly, but more likely a lack of understanding, I shortly found myself toying with the idea of a drink. The thought of just smoking a little bit of a joint also sounded appealing. Afterall, I had arrived. Had I not? I in no way was able to make the connection between not drinking and using drugs with the rapid and profound improvement of my life. Some in AA call this the mental blank spot, which is the alcoholic's inability to recall the misery caused by alcohol in the not-so-distant past. That was a paraphrase from the actual description given in AA's Big Book (the commonly used term for the official text, *Alcoholics Anonymous* used in the fellowship). Nonetheless, eleven and a half months into a one-year commitment to prove to myself I was not a problem drinker or drug user, found me with a joint in lips. I was completely satisfied with the excuses I made to justify my using before reaching my goal. Maybe there was some unconscious drive there which intuitively knew that if I made it the full year, it would have been worse for me in the long run, in terms of guilt and shame… or maybe I am overthinking it! Maybe it was simply the obsession of the mind discussed in AA literature which prevents the alcoholic from staying stopped when they commit to stopping the drinking and/or drug use. Maybe it is something else, but what is paramount is that my thinking had led me back on the road to ruin.

Following about another year's worth of alcohol and drug driven turmoil, I found myself in the graces of my loving sister. My sister whom I cannot thank enough for doing the hardest thing someone who loves an alcoholic or addict can do. She cut me off and stopped enabling me. I know this must have been exceedingly difficult for her as I was forced to live in my car following her setting of the boundary which put an end to my taking advantage of her love. This was also the spark which would ignite my fire of sobriety. Of course, within a few weeks from that moment, I would get myself fired from another job, and go on a 5-day blackout over the New Year. I also squandered all but $20 of the severance I was provided to get me back on my feet during those 5 days.

It seemed that I had finally hit the bottom they talk about in the 12-step programs. From a mental health perspective, it would seem as I had hit bottom, because I thought killing myself might be a good solution to my current predicament. Do not get me wrong, I had played the suicide card several times before in order to manipulate someone into getting what I wanted, as many alcoholics and addicts are prone to do. Please do not be shocked if you are of the uninitiated. To the addict it is survival, and nothing is below doing what needs to be done to acquire the relief which is drinking and using. The main difference this time is that I was the only one there and I was not trying to manipulate someone. This time it was for real. Though the thought of suicide and accompanying feeling were quickly fleeting, *it was real.* That scared me.

The realness of the ideation scared me because I had a plan to go along with it, not that I was aware of what that meant from a profession perspective at that time of course. Nonetheless, I may have pessimism to thank, because part of the reason I did not go through with it was that I thought I would mess that up too... end up a paraplegic not dead. The other and more likely thing that kept me from doing it was my Catholic upbringing, which I mistakenly claimed as oppressive and the like throughout my adulthood. I thought to myself, no heaven for me if I commit suicide... What if it *is* true? The possible implications were too much. I can thank my mother for that influence, which incidentally was helpful in connecting with a higher power in my quest for sobriety. Anyways... I ended up trying to formulate another plan other than killing myself.

After some time and investigation, the light bulb in my head went off... "I'll go to rehab." It seems, at least at that point in time, that treatment centers are not all that helpful when a person does not have any money or insurance. Nonetheless they gave me a list of AA meetings in the area. I chose one to go to. Following a series of several unlikely circumstances, a fellow that I used to run with in my youth was at that meeting. He told me that he had been sober for about one and a half years. I thought to myself… "If he could do it, I could do it. After all… he was way worse than me." I make this statement with tongue in cheek! It is a testament to the distorted thinking which many (I dare not say *all*) alcoholics/addicts use to continue their behavior.

Thus, started my journey to sobriety and a sober lifestyle. On that journey, much time is spent initiating what the 12-step programs, AA in particular, describe as a spiritual awakening. To some people, this causes bristling antagonism as they say in the Big Book. To others it simply may be a misunderstanding which needs clarification. To me, it is deeply personal to each person who experiences it. What I can say I believe is true to all those who experience it, is that it is *freedom*. The spiritual awakening is described as a complete upheaval and rearrangement of one's previous convictions and beliefs, again paraphrasing the Big Book. This spiritual awakening or psychic change as it is also described is what transforms the substance afflicted from a selfish, self-seeking, egotistical and (by the point of seeking help) miserable individual into a giving and altruistic being, in most cases. I believe that this is also in line with the one of the goals of psychology and the mental health field. The goal of transforming an unsatisfactory state of existence into a satisfying one. Please note that this is a somewhat simplified assessment. The common ideas of what aid a person in attaining satisfaction will be discussed as we proceed through the different philosophies presented in the text, as well as how they align with 12-Step recovery.

My motivation for continuing my education and training to become a mental health profession was two-fold. First and foremost, I believed, and still believe that I may be able to have a larger impact on recovery from substances as a psychologist and engaging this population as such. Second, I had wanted to be a psychologist since high school because I had a desire to find out what was *wrong* with me. That... I found out in AA. What was wrong with me, that is. Again, I write this with tongue in cheek. The other thing I found out in AA was that engaging in actions I did not want to engage in and living by principles is what helped heal me and countless others.

As I embarked on my professional journey into the field of mental health, I discovered that many of the principles I had learned getting sober in AA are prevalent in the psychological philosophies which rule the day. This was exciting. However, what was not exciting or encouraging was what seemed to be the mental health industries seeming incompetence in blending the two to develop an effective treatment environment for alcoholics/addicts. This then became a primary motivation in the undertaking of writing this volume. I hope to provide a framework and understanding for those who are not familiar with 12-step recovery. More so, to give a glimpse into the lifestyle with which the alcoholic and addict identifies, in the hope therapists and counselors may better connect with this population. I hope to build a bridge which links the psychological truths of 12-step recovery with the intention of increasing clinical efficacy. I also hope to decrease some of the professional and academic contempt I believe and have experienced exists for AA and 12-step programs. At the very least, I hope this work provides an interesting and informative read for anyone interested in the subject. With that… I hope you enjoy the time you spend with this work.

In reverence for AA, many of the principles I learned, which saved and transformed my life are also present in psychological philosophies. My hope in sharing is to assist people in making these connections, possibly reducing AA scrutiny in the academic community, and assisting professionals working in the field in incorporating these ideas in a productive way. My intention is to be as helpful as possible so that we can guide as many people as possible to recovery from whatever they are powerless over. Whatever that may be, alcohol, drugs, a behavior or their emotions. Finally, in respect for the tradition of anonymity at the level of press, radio and films with the intention to protect the society which freed me and so many others, I author this book using my first name and last initials only. I do not speak for Alcoholics Anonymous. Again, I only seek to be helpful and provide the insight of my experience, strength, and hope.

Treatment Centers and Alcoholics Anonymous

For those unfamiliar with the origins of Alcoholics Anonymous, I will briefly describe how AA was formed. This is a non-detailed description given to generally familiarize those who are uniformed of this beginning. As a member of the society, I highly recommend reading <u>Dr. Bob and the Good Old-timers,</u> as well as <u>Pass It On</u> for those interested in how the program and fellowship was born. These are the stories of the founding fathers, Dr. Bob and Bill W. in their quest to find a solution to their problem with alcohol, while unknowingly creating the foundations of a worldwide movement. They are fascinating reads and may help the therapist and newcomer who is uninitiated in learning the concepts, as well as the lingo that is commonly used throughout the rooms of AA and other 12 step programs. Many in the fellowship believe a divine motivation behind the forming of the 12 steps and upon completion of the readings, one may be inclined to agree. This is especially true when considering the nature of the alcoholic's behavior and attitude, coupled with the limited means of carrying their message in the age of primitive telecommunications.

So, back to the origins. Alcoholics Anonymous was not the first movement aimed at assuaging suffering alcoholics from the grips of active alcoholism. An earlier movement was a group known as the

Washingtonians, who started to have some success with alcoholics by using spiritual means. The success they were having begun to gain some notoriety and soon they expanded their focus to other "moral degenerations." As a result, the Washingtonian group found that their message became diluted and ineffective, eventually leading to their demise. This is the basis of the tradition of "singleness of purpose," which will be discussed a bit more broadly in short.

The Oxford Group was a Christian movement of the early 1900's which also had some success with alcoholics. This was a group that Bill encountered and began attending to find a solution to his alcohol problem. The Oxford Group used a treatment program devised of six steps in which the general objectives included, confess, repent and make restitution. These were a few of the tenants which Bill thought disagreeable, not simply for him, but for alcoholics in general which were later addressed in the forming of Alcoholic Anonymous' 12 Steps. Despite these disagreements, the Oxford Group's tenants did aid Bill in making some progress in dealing with his drinking, yet he could not find a way to remain "dry" completely. As such, Bill came to view the concepts as useful, but believed that for the alcoholic to make use of them productively some adjustment was needed.

Bill remained true to his convictions until he was on a business trip in the mid-west. Bill had been on a good "dry" spell, had returned to work and was again building a hopeful outlook for his future. This was not an unfamiliar pattern for Bill and those who are familiar with the toils of alcoholism and addiction. Many are able to recover for a brief period but cannot remain abstinent as they succumb to trivial excuses to imbibe "one more time" despite understanding what the likely outcome of such an action will bring about for them. This again is a description of the previously mentioned idea of the "mental blank spot" which leads to relapse.

One evening, upon the conclusion of a successful day of work in that mid-western town, Bill strolled across the hotel lobby and his attention was caught by the lively sounds coming out of the bar. At this time, he was confronted by the thought that a drink would be a good idea, as the day had been such a success. Even though to this point in his life he had never successfully consumed "just one drink." Notwithstanding, the belief that he could remained (mental blank spot). Panic stricken, Bill searched the phone book for some relief, at which point he came across the number for some members of the Oxford Group.

This is where Bill met Dr. Bob who was also an alcoholic of some repute in the local area. Bill discovered that his obsession to drink dissipated when discussing all he had learned about sobriety with another who was suffering from alcoholism. In providing the aid needed by the other person, Bill found relief in his own desire to drink, thus laying the groundwork for the idea that one alcoholic helping another may provide a solution to the alcoholic condition. Though Dr. Bob did not remain sober following this initial meeting, Bill did. This fact would have been lost on Bill had it not been for his wife who pointed it out to him. Bill believed himself unsuccessful in the endeavor, as Dr. Bob did not remain sober. However, shortly following that experience, Dr.

Bob did find long term sobriety becoming the cofounder of Alcoholics Anonymous. From this encounter, sprang the idea that one alcoholic could remain sober by discussing with another alcoholic the things they had learned and done to achieve sobriety, whether the other remain abstinent or not. This idea would become the foundation through which the AA fellowship would snowball into the most successful treatment program available for alcohol and substance abusers, in my opinion.

Sadly, as AA is an anonymous program, it is difficult to acquire accurate numbers to reflect where treatment/recovery success has been achieved. Given the nature of the AA traditions and how that reflects on the concept of anonymity, there is a healthy suspicion of anyone who may be, for instance, taking notes during the process of the meeting or of someone conducting a survey. As far as the traditions are concerned this skepticism is especially acute in the setting of the closed meetings, which are for "those who have identified as an alcoholic or have a desire to stop drinking."

That said, Bill provided some statistical information regarding AA's treatment success in plain view as described in the forward to the second edition of the Big Book (Alcoholics Anonymous, 2001. Pp. xx). Of course, this seems far from the scientific method now followed in the realm of social sciences. However, one must not forget that case study is also a form of research used in the social sciences today. Also, it is not unlikely, especially in the early days, that Bill would have wanted to sell the idea or at least the recovery method for alcoholism to the highest bidder. He was a businessman after all, and his entrepreneurial spirit was strong. Bill being a stockbroker and "numbers man," it would not be unlikely that he would have tried to keep as accurate a record as possible without violating the identities of AA's early members. It is not too far to imagine that initially this may have been his motivation, thus lending deeper credence to these initial recovery estimations. However, it is equally apparent that something changed Bill's mind in this regard, as the fellowship and his sobriety grew. It is possible that something bigger than Bill removed Bill's will and worldly desire from him, while still leaving a rough estimate of recovery successes in the aftermath. He is a great example of how one's values and humility change through the process of recovery and a psychic change.

With the prior statement in mind about the changes in Bill, I will veer off the current focus for a moment. There is a consensus among members of 12-step that there are three levels or types of sobriety: physical, emotional, and spiritual. The *process* of having a spiritual awakening, also known as a psychic change, moves through these different states of sobriety as the person grows in the program. With that said, the alcoholic, Bill in this specific instance, likely had a change of heart between 1939 and 1955. It is not that difficult to hypothesize from my experience as both an alcoholic (sober by way of AA) and psychologist that this is the case. Earlier editions of the "Grapevine," a soft bound monthly magazine distributed by AA's Central Office, has articles written by Bill highlighting his struggles with this "worldliness" and drive to be a "top man" throughout his sobriety.

Returning to the prior focus of treatment success; assuming, these numbers are even partially accurate, it would indicate a vastly improved estimation of one's chances for recovery versus today's treatment environment in my experience. Despite ethical constraints and quite possibly legal violations, as an accurate percentage is likely unattainable, to make such a suggestion is considered misleading. Nonetheless, treatment centers these days boast success rates of 40-50% on their websites. First off, though I do not have statistical backing to make the next claim, I am comfortable in saying that numbers this high, except in a few rare cases, are largely fictitious. I worked with an MSW, who worked at a highly reputable treatment center employing an intricate alumni program; their estimates of recovery successes were at something like 25-30%. What is more, this center has hired an independent investigator to reveal and process the numbers. This is not the norm, as most of the treatment centers I have worked and have researched rely on in house alumni contact coordinators to make phone calls checking on prior patient's progress in continued care. I imagine the phone interview goes something like this... "Hello. This is XYZ recovery. Are you still clean and sober?" Alumnus responds, "Aaah... Why yes, ***of course*** I am." I am surprised that the advertised success rates are that low, again speaking with tongue in cheek. A 50% percent advertised success rate is likely the safest number in terms of the ethical and legal issues inherent in making such claims. The person either stays sober or they don't-50%! No misinformation there... But I digress.

A research project directed by the National Institute on Alcohol

Abuse and Alcoholism yielded some interesting results. Project Match (1997) was a multi-site research endeavor which sought less to measure treatment effectiveness than it did to seek treatment compatibility between modalities and patients. There were three modalities included in the project; 1) 12 step-based treatment, 2) Cognitive based models, and 3) Motivational Enhancement Therapy, designed to "roll with the resistance."

Although treatment effectiveness was not a primary focus of this study, it was noted that outpatients who received 12-step philosophies/treatment were more likely to remain completely abstinent in the year following treatment than outpatients in the other treatments. In terms of the findings which this project was seeking, it was noted that individuals who were high in religiosity/spirituality and those indicating they were seeking meaning in their lives generally did better with the 12-step philosophy. Outpatients with high levels of psychopathology, on the other hand, did not thrive in the 12-step focused treatment.

Wallace, 2005 brought to light a few criticisms of Project Match. One being the exclusion of participants if they were dependent on cocaine or heroin, used drugs intravenously (these seem appropriate, as the study was conducted by a center focused on alcoholism and alcohol abuse), were suicidal or had acute psychosis. However, those excluded characteristics are all part of the general treatment center populations and all part of the makeup of those in 12-step societies as well. If anything, a more acutely symptomatic population might have bolstered the numbers for the 12-step programs, as the idea of "hitting bottom" or a state of hopelessness tends to be viewed as a strength from the 12-step perspective. This will be better exemplified by a later discussion of the alcohol abuser versus the "real alcoholic." Of course, this is not to say that 12-step programs do not work for someone who has yet to "hit bottom." However, the literature and experience of case studies does indicate that many who benefit from the 12-step recovery philosophy are running out of second chances. The aforementioned exclusion of IV and "hard" drug users is an illustration, though likely unintentional, of the idea of singleness of purpose which again will be discussed more deeply in short.

As if we did not need another reason to scratch our heads in terms of measuring effectiveness in treatment modalities. Government funded research in this area no longer measures *effectiveness* as a person's ability to maintain abstinence (Addiction Treatment, 2008). What is more, in some instances, simply remaining in a treatment center is considered a success. Facts like this get my medical model conspiracy "spider sense tingling," but I digress.

Notwithstanding, to employ the open mind that is discussed and exemplified as a useful tool in recovery and is a focal point in the 12-step program, the harm reduction model measures success by… well yes, reduction of harm. As such, from this perspective, a heroin addict who switches to moderate alcohol use is measured as a success. I guess, when viewed through an open mind, *that* reduction is… "better."

Although the diagnostic criteria and nomenclature has changed in the Diagnostic and Statistical Manual of Mental Disorders-V

(DSM-V), in the previous DSM-VI there used to be a little thing called progression/tolerance involved in making the diagnosis. Progression states in a general manner, that if a person is inclined to addiction, dependence (DSM-IV) or substance use disorders (DSM-V) then the type or amount of substances a person uses will eventually need to be increased or changed to something stronger. Hence, if a person is prone to satisfy their addiction (the mental and physical) using opiates, and they try to satisfy that propensity with alcohol; progression will intervene, and logic would indicate that eventually they will either drink to oblivion or return to their drug of choice. Ask anyone who has been in the 12-step society for a significant period and they will be able to tell and retell this story of progression. The Big Book cites, "Here are some of the methods we have tried" with the goal of reducing harm. They include, drinking only beer, limiting the number of drinks, switching from scotch to brandy... (Alcoholics Anonymous, 2001. Pp.31). To surmise, this is the reason why the harm reduction model, in terms of the *true* addict or alcoholic as will be described will ultimately fail.

To lend further credence, though I have seen and heard the scenario repeatedly, one patient I worked with crystallized this belief in my memory. A young lady and her family, whom I worked with for over a year and a half considered herself at one-point to be a heroin addict. That point was her first time in treatment for her addiction. She was proposed the harm reduction model but did not buy in to the idea; *at first.* Shortly following the completion of the program, she was attending, she succumbed to the obsession so articulately illustrated in the AA Big Book. Eventually, she convinced herself that she could have the proverbial "one drink." Not immediately, but not long after she became so dependent on, or drank in such a disordered manner (forgive my cynicism) that she was in the same bind. Paraphrasing her words, she described the scenario as actually being worse off than when she was using heroin as a drug of choice. This eventually led to her loosing custody of her young daughter. That in my opinion is not reducing harm.

Fortunately, through the course of treatment in the clinic in which I and others worked with this young lady; abstinence has begun to remedy that situation. Last we worked together, she was in the process of regaining full custody of her child who ended up in, if you can believe, a more harmful situation with the father and her father's dysfunctional family system.

Yes... this is only one story. With that said, it is one of many I have heard in the rooms of Alcoholics Anonymous of a similar nature. Oh, yes... and I am only one individual. In keeping with the open mindedness professed in 12-step principles, the preceding story is about the nature of the *true* or *real* alcoholic or addict. I think the harm reduction model may work when one is dealing with the moderate or maybe even the heavy substance abuser. However, I would argue that in most cases, once that individual has reached the treatment center level of care that the question of severity has been answered.

In assessing a person's alcohol or drug use and whether it is problematic or not, the psychological fraternity has one method and

AA's "Big Book" has another. In the preceding paragraph I mentioned the "true alcoholic" as illustrated in the "Big Book." I also spoke of the moderated drinker for whom the harm reduction model may be an option. In terms of drug use, there is likely a class who could be considered recreational users. I think this might be so for substances like marijuana, cocaine and some prescription drugs, but not so for heroin. I will explain more later. So, what is the difference between the "true" alcoholic/addict versus the moderate imbiber?

In the chapter "The Doctor's Opinion" (Alcoholics Anonymous, 2001), Dr. Silkworth, who was a pioneer in the treatment of alcohol and drug addiction, attempts to address and classify types of alcoholics while admitting it was beyond the scope of the book. It seems he believed that it was less important to what or how one was addicted and thusly labeled, than he was concerned about finding a way to recover. Nonetheless, he briefly describes five common types he had experienced in his work. The first was the psychopath, described as being over-remorseful, making lots of promises, but never a decision to act. Next is the type of person who is unwilling to admit that he or she has a problem. This person is constantly adjusting their lives to fit alcohol in. Third is the person who constantly believes that after being free from alcohol for a time he or she could again take a drink. When they do, disaster followed. This person is also known as a "periodic." Forth is the "Manic-Depressive (aka Bipolar)." Silkworth surmises that this person is the least understood by their friends and that an entire chapter could be written on them alone. Needless to say, entire books have been written about them today. Lastly, there is the person who seems completely normal, except where the effects of alcohol on him or her is concerned. Silkworth identified one symptom in common with all these types, as well as the types not included, which is what he called the "phenomenon of craving." He likens it to an allergy, which is an apt description. Furthermore, he stated that this phenomenon is what differentiates alcoholics from other people. Case study evidence he presents includes stories about how people who had been working on certain business deals or the like; would take a drink a few days before closing it and end up never making the grade, so to speak. He and any other "true alcoholic" is likely to confirm this idea. It is not about overcoming some form of mental control or incorporating the A-B-C model of cognitive behavioral theory. It is about having and needing to overcome a craving which is physical and coupled with equally powerful obsessions. As such, he supported the idea of abstinence, as no other remedy had been found to that date. I would argue that this remains true today where the true alcoholic or addict is concerned.

Though there have been some physiological discoveries since that time, none have been truly significant in terms of changing the nature of alcoholism and addiction, in my experience and opinion. Of course, we can link family history, but that again is a question of nature versus nurture. Neurobiology has provided clues and indications of where brain activity is significantly changed or different, such as in the Amygdala. However, to the date in which this was written and to the best of my knowledge, there is no genetic marker found in the DNA strand which says… alcoholic, or addict.

Silkworth, in the section he wrote for the "Big Book" at AA's request, describes alcoholics as people who are addicted to alcohol. I emphasize this because for whatever reason (likely the AA tradition of "singleness of purpose") in today's recovery environment an addict generally refers to a person who is addicted to opiates/opioids, heroin and "drugs" more specifically. There is also the possibility that this is simply a quirk of the drug culture. In addition, because of the aforementioned tradition, the uninitiated newcomer who identifies in AA as simply an "addict" is often confused when a veteran member asks, "Do you have a desire to stop drinking?" Many misinterpret this as an offense and distort the intent to forego group attendance and the beneficial support because of it. I have seen a softening of this policy in the sense of how it is enacted in recent times. Driven by an intent to be of utmost help in people's recovery, the newcomer is often taken aside and taught the tradition of "singleness of purpose" and the reason why it is so important.

Others confuse this with the idea that AA or any other Anonymous programs are only for those with whatever specific ailment is described by the letter preceding the second "A." That is not the case. It is simply a way to reduce the risk of diluting the message and suffering the fate of the Washingtonian and Oxford groups before. Therefore, the discussion focus is contained to "problems related to alcoholism." In that context, it is not inappropriate to discuss other substance and/or process addictions when prefaced with a statement of that intent. For instance, "I know this is a meeting of AA, but… has also been a problem because of my drinking."

Another fundamental problem with the harm reduction model is the physiological aspect of alcoholism and addiction. As my personal recovery experience is in the AA program, the main idea of abstinence is summed in the saying, "one drink (or whatever may fit) is too many and one hundred is not enough." What that essentially means is when somebody prone to substance abuse ingests a substance, a physiological phenomenon occurs which triggers the manifestation of craving. Craving, as experienced by the alcoholic or addict is not a casual wanting or urge. In these individuals a simple craving can grow into an obsessiveness which blocks reason and leads to many cognitive distortions, if not delusions (mental blank spot). These delusions can lead otherwise reasonable people to believe that despite all the evidence to the contrary, they *can* have and *will* only have… one drink. Dr. Silkworth, the author of "The Doctor's Opinion" section in the AA Big Book, observes and labels this phenomenon as an "allergy." Roughly defined, an allergy is an abnormal reaction of the body to an introduced allergen. As body and mind are connected to behavior, many an alcoholic or addict would agree that the idea of being allergic to substances would explain a lot. Especially why they are the ones who experience the adverse effects of what started out as a casual night of drinking and their companions are not. It may also explain some old sayings and ideas associated with alcoholics, such as, "Drink just doesn't agree with her" or "Why can't he just take it or leave it, like everyone else."

This idea of an allergy is not far off, in my opinion, as anyone familiar with the phenomenon I am discussing will attest. There is an adverse side effect displayed in the alcoholic or addict who ingests a mind-altering substance. Maybe someday physicians and research scientists may find the link beyond a doubt, but as of today there is only smoke. But often, where there is smoke, there is fire. Lastly, this idea of an allergy can be used today as a coping and protective mechanism for individuals seeking refrain from their substance use disorders. Counselors encourage these individuals to assert an allergy if questioned about their drinking when called to unavoidable high-risk situations, such as weddings or other types of congregations where libations will be flowing. "Would you like a drink?" "No thank you. I am allergic to alcohol."

So, what differentiates the moderate user from the "real" substance abuser has been discussed, at least in the eyes of the 12-step perspective. Control is what differentiates the two. Well, loss of control to be more accurate. Why does one lose that control? That is a guiding and difficult question to answer thus far in the discussion. Many physiological relationships have been found in alcoholism and addiction, but as of yet, no definitive or unquestioned cause. Nearly a century ago, Dr. Silkworth, through his observation of hundreds of individuals coming to him for treatment was able to postulate a physical connection which he described as an allergy triggered by using mind-altering substances.

Then, this allergy manifested in a physical and mental craving, coupled with obsessions which eventually led the person to destructive alcohol or substance abuse.

From my personal case files, also known as my experience, comes this story. The leader of the meeting was a late 50's early 60's-ish woman, who spoke about not having her first drink until 2010. She spoke of losing a son in the Middle East war and was able to deal with that in her own way, as she owned her own business and kept busy at it, a classic avoidance technique. However, when her other son was gravely injured in a related war, she began to drink (2010). She reported that that within 6 months of beginning to drink, she began to have adverse outcomes, namely a DUI. Though, she committed to refrain from drink, she nevertheless received two more arrests which subsequently landed her in AA. This story also illustrates an idea discussed in AA which suggests that, given the progressive nature of alcoholism, when a person is prone to alcoholism or abstains then relapses, they start off at the point which they would have been if they did not stop drinking at all. This story also suggests some form of physiological phenomenon in action.

The woman described in the case study started drinking in her late 50's or there about and displayed symptoms of advanced alcoholism in a rather short time, as if she had started drinking earlier in life and experienced progression. Additionally, the AA big book includes a case study in which a successful young businessman began having undesirable consequences as a result of his drinking. He was able to assert himself and not drink again until retirement and a successful career. With the intent of once again enjoying a relaxing drink or two, this man found himself quickly in the throes of alcoholism and shortly there afterward hospitalized. Just a side note on hospitalization in the old days. The hospitalization often meant going to an asylum, not some mansion, overlooking the ocean with personal chefs! So, what I am saying is that it was somewhat less desirable to relapse in those days, which could have also been a motivational factor against relapse.

Treatment centers provide a relatively safe place for individuals to begin recovery. For cases in which a high risk of harm during detox exists, clinical intervention can be imperative. For the highly motivated individual who has experienced a significant amount of pain and is willing to adhere to clinical direction, there is a good chance of recovering. However, there are covert dangers lurking in the environments of treatment centers as well. In the years that I have been working in addiction treatment and recovery clinics I have witnessed some discouraging events. These events coupled with inconsistent disciplinary actions which can cause one to question the motivations behind them, has left me at times wondering if I am a part of the problem or a part of the solution where working in a treatment center is concerned.

There seem to be a good number of patients who have learned how to manipulate the system in a way that becomes a lifestyle. Even more frustrating is the knowledge that less than ethical parties have facilitated the relapse of individuals, in order to re-admit said patient at a higher level of care which commands a higher revenue for the treatment center.

Other times, patients know and understand that if they relapse, even without coercion, they will be re-admitted to treatment. This then becomes the cycle, rather than a cycle which builds efficacy and esteem through actions which merit such; like getting a job and paying one's way, for instance.

Often these manipulative people model or teach the maladaptive behaviors to the individual who may be motivated to make a real attempt at achieving sobriety. In a highly vulnerable state, these individuals often capitulate to what they believe to be an "easier softer way" which has been a hallmark of their life choices to this point. A concept in AA and 12-step recovery societies is the idea that alcoholics and addicts are seeking to cut corners in most aspects of their lives, hence an "easier, softer way." What the specifics of the easier way entail may be in question, for instance easing emotional pain or maybe financial gain. Either way, it seems clear that alcoholics and addicts are seeking a short cut to something. Dependent personality types, as well as others exist who make a lifestyle out of treatment. For a variety of reasons, from a psychosocial perspective beyond the aforementioned personality types, a substantial number of individuals engage in a circular pattern of entering treatment; regaining some physical health while disregarding psychological health; eventually they relapse thus starting the process again.

It appears as if insurance companies have begun to become wise to this phenomenon and have adjusted accordingly. Notwithstanding, I still hear about patients who come into treatment following a half dozen or more previous attempts at recovery. It may seem I am not being grateful, as job security seems abundant. However, this is not why I became a therapist. I thought my recovery experience coupled with therapy techniques may help reduce the number of those suffering from alcoholism and addiction in the world. I believe I have played a part in the recovery of many of my clients. The frustration is that it sometimes seems as if I and other therapists I have worked with are swimming upstream against a river of insurance companies and CEO's.

In many cases, the identities of people in recovery are strongly influenced by their alcoholic and addiction-oriented lifestyles. AA's Big Book speaks of being driven by delusions and illusions. Many of these false ideas are related to a person's substance abuse behaviors. Whether a person is an artist and believes that creativity is linked to the use of substances, a businessman who drinks to relieve the stress of a day's wheeling's and dealings, or a student whose compromised self-esteem is boosted by a nip or puff. These narratives develop into mistaken beliefs about whom a person is. These misconceptions often fuel using and relapse behavior. They are often so deeply entrenched that recovery seems to be like an identity crisis. What is more, the identity fights back to defend the threat that sobriety poses, psychodynamically speaking. This is the dilemma for many who try to recover from substance abuse; the pain drinking and using is creating in a person's life versus the emotional pain of deconstructing then re-creating a person's identity.

Another problem which exists in treatment centers with a purely psychological orientation is the previously mentioned concept of

"Harm Reduction." The harm reduction model, in a nutshell, posits that reduction of addictive behaviors is the road to recovery. Yet when considering the physiological aspects previously discussed about the "true" alcoholic or addict, it would seem at the very least a difficult proposal in terms of efficacy of treatment.

As far as the physiological mechanisms of absorption and activation go between alcohol and drugs is outside the scope and focus of this book. However, as far as identity is concerned in the recovery community, it seems to a certain degree (usually the first 6 months) that addicts do not want to be labeled alcoholics and vice versa. However, when considering Dr. Silkworth's reverence, his statement that he oversaw a hospital which treats those who are afflicted with alcoholic **addiction** can be used to appease anyone who seeks argument. Notwithstanding, this may be a significant and valid topic which would and could spur a larger discussion. A discussion which may argue that differences which stem from genetic markers between addiction and alcoholism or whether these afflictions are born of nature or nurture and of course, which addiction is the worst or most lethal. All this contention which creates division and strife is cast aside in 12-step societies, for the principled statement which has saved many lives, "Look for the similarities, not the differences." That statement is the beginning of the journey in the opening of one's mind and in moving towards acceptance of both self and others. This journey ends with peace of mind, something many in the world seek, yet do not find.

Besides the harm reduction model philosophy, another drawback in clinics, or more accurately, the reason I believe the clinical treatment field is failing is largely due to the emphasis on "empirically supported interventions." I know this may seem counterintuitive on the surface but let me explain. It is not that I think empirical support is not important, as it is the main if not only type of "proof" we can muster in psychology. There are many arguments that can be made as related to the ability to bend statistics to fit the intended outcome, but I digress… The issue is not with the interventions themselves, but the emphasis on bombarding the individual with them all at once.

The patient comes in from the street or wherever. This person has likely tried and failed to achieve sobriety several times and is trying to find a way to stop using drugs and alcohol. Again, here I include a presumption that they want to stop and stay stopped. As mentioned earlier, many are seeking other methods, such as drinking or using "like a gentleman." Maybe, some of these newly sober individuals are actually seeking abstinence initially, but when they hear that if they just cut down or switch from vodka to beer and can lead a satisfying life, they decide abstinence is too drastic. Again, harm reduction may be an option for some, but when considering the chronic, hardcore alcoholic or drug addict, experience indicates this idea to be folly.

When considering the problem with empirically backed interventions, the problem is not the intervention themselves. "Well then," one is inclined to ask, "What is the problem?" I argue that the problem is in timing. This timing is often pressed by eager clinical directors, who are likely being pressured by C.O.O.'s and C.E.O.'s to meet the criteria required by the insurance companies to get paid. As such, therapists are often pressured to include an abundance of important and useful topics that have empirical backing. However, this disregards the principle and significance of timing in providing effective psychotherapy. The question as to a person's readiness for (name intervention) at the time is ignored. This, in and of itself, is often detrimental when considering the concept of risk versus resiliencies.

Information is great, do not get me wrong. I would not have continued my education to get a Psy.D. if I did not believe it so. However, all the information presented in my graduate and post graduate education and training went against one of the most important principles I learned getting sober. "Keep it simple." All the different avenues of psychology and recovery may present complication for the one who may yet harbor reservations for their recovery. When presented with ideas, interventions or other avenues that do not include abstinence, these individuals are likely run with it. Often running with the belief that their drinking and using careers would have been or will be different given this newly learned concept. Concepts such as CBT, DBT, defense mechanism's and the like are all important ideas to understand and internalize, however I also believe that one must figure out how to stay sober before these concepts will be useful. The self-manipulation of placing faith in a psychological ideal versus the thought of abstinence more often than not leads to detrimental results such as relapse.

To reiterate, not all concepts presented in treatment are untimely, for instance meditation and mindfulness. The idea of the 11th step which seeks to increase one's spiritual connection through prayer and meditation is said to be the one step which can be taken out of order. Health and wellness, an extremely popular group topic in recovery centers may illustrate both effective and ineffective concepts. For instance, exercise is particularly important in early recovery as this is a way to counteract Post-Acute Withdrawal Syndrome, which in general is associated with one's brain chemistry resetting to a more homeostatic state. Exercise is known to increase neurotransmitter production and can be helpful for those who have been relying on substances to do that job for the last months or years. On the other hand, quitting smoking may not be the best idea.

Often, people get on what is called "the pink cloud." The pink cloud could be likened to a light mania, shortly following the start of sobriety, where the individual is so struck by all the positivity that they have experienced and the improvement in their physical health, that the want to quit and change everything about their lives all at once. These newly sober individuals become obsessed with wanting to eat right, wanting to apologize to everyone and often wanting to do whatever is necessary to obtain optimum health. What is the problem with this you ask? The ambition is not necessarily "bad," if you will. However, the ineffectiveness lies in the dynamic of engaging in old over-compensatory behavior. Alcoholics and drug addicts often over-promise and/or over-extend themselves in a somewhat anxiety driven endeavor of making up for lost time or making up for lost dreams and expectations. Sadly, this making up process could have less to do with their lost dreams and expectations versus the lost dreams and expectations of others. The newly sober individual is in a process of recreating their identities and may take regrettable actions during these "pink cloud" moments. That is the essence of the 12-step motto, "Easy does it."

A final point of contention (for now) where treatment centers, or more specifically, those who run the curriculums of these treatment centers fall short is in how they identify with the patient. I understand from a scholastic and therapeutic perspective that one need not suffer from an affliction to be helpful in treating a said affliction. But to the people afflicted with alcoholism or addiction, this identification seems like kind of a big deal. This appears to be true, more so than in dual diagnosis populations than in non-dual diagnosis populations, in my experience. Maybe it is a defensive type of phenomenon, but it seems that alcoholics and addicts always ask about the therapist's drinking and drug histories. "Are you an addict or alcoholic?" Whether or not the therapist can identify with the patient's pain, experiences and discomfort, *as an alcoholic or addict* becomes paramount, even though it should not. Again, this is an observation from experience. This is not true of all client's and what the total solution is, I do not know. Yet I do know the language that is used in therapy can help strengthen the therapeutic relationship. I hope this work may be helpful in some way by lending some insight to those who counsel these individuals in this regard.

Taking the idea of one's identity to another level, one must consider the impact of repeatedly engaging in self-talk (therapeutically speaking, one's internal dialogue) which reinforces the identity associated with the alcoholic/addict lifestyle. There seems to be several associated actions and beliefs that emerge with being a "member" of this class. The power of ritual becomes a strong binder in the cement of continued drinking and using. One's identity becomes embroiled in a conflict with their ego which is threatened when presented with the idea of getting sober. All this psychodynamic fodder clouds the reality of the trouble and unproductive consequences which is at the forefront of advancing substance dependence… or substance use disorder if you prefer. It becomes such a delusion; the way life *is,* versus the way the alcoholic/addict *believes* life is, that recovery becomes even more difficult. With this in mind, the therapist attempts to change the patient's associated narrative in this regard. As a result of said beliefs and actions, coupled with maladaptive results and relationships, stigma is created about problem drinkers and drug users.

In the hope of reducing stigma, it seems a growing trend by therapists, non-alcoholic/addict therapists, is the idea of not calling these individuals alcoholics or addicts. They believe the stigma and shame that these titles carry is detrimental to their recovery, which may be true. However, these same professions often seem to have no problem in attaching other debilitating labels (anxious, depressed, traumatized etc.) as related to their mental health diagnosis to those in treatment for a said disorder. I wonder what the difference is, but I digress. My experience with labeling myself an alcoholic was quite the opposite.

As previously discussed, it is apparent that those with problematic substance abuse due to their actions and beliefs form an identity as related to the terms, alcoholic and/or addict. This imposed narrative becomes an instruction book if you will. An instruction book on how to act and how to think, "because I'm an… (fill in the blank with whatever disorder you must), I have to act… (again, fill in the blank with whatever behavior is causing distress) this way." This serves as a distortion of the reality which continued substance abuse is creating in the life of the afflicted.

The cycle of immediate relief of substances, followed by inevitable consequences is disregarded due to the allusiveness of the relief which is experienced through the substance use. In other words, it becomes their coping mechanism. From this perspective it is understandable why many therapists can see this as a hinderance. I have engaged in this dynamic myself, using the moniker, "alcoholic" as an excuse for my behavior. "Sorry, but I'm an alcoholic." However, the crux of whether these terms are strengths or weaknesses lies in the *understanding and meaning* the person associates with these terms. The meaning the alcoholic or addict creates in their life narratives related to these labels becomes paramount.

I will help clarify this, again using my personal experience of the process in my own recovery. I have also shared this same phenomenological experience with others in recovery, though they may not be aware as it is simply a part of the recovery process in the 12-step societies. As stated in the closing of the last paragraph, my narrative and understanding of what it meant to be an alcoholic or addict was used to perpetuate my maladaptive behaviors. Without a doubt this would fall into the weakness category. One of the mistaken beliefs I had regarding this was the idea that I could stop whenever I wanted to stop. This was true to a certain extent, as whenever the consequences got bad enough, I would stop. The problem was that I could not stay stopped despite the obvious improvements in my life and relationships. The idea that I wanted to stop *permanently* would get buried in my unconscious somewhere and the overwhelming obsession that I could have one drink or smoke one joint would return. I would succumb and the cycle would begin again.

Having been left with no more ideas, or being beaten into a state of reasonableness, as is commonly stated in meetings, I arrived at AA's doorstep. They presented the idea of a physical malady, also known as an allergy, coupled with the obsessions of the mind as an explanation of why I could not stay stopped (sober, abstinent) or have one drink. Do not get me wrong, I have drunk moderately at times, though I did not enjoy it. These instances were, upon reflection with sponsors, sober friends, and my therapist, simply actions designed to *prove* the mistaken idea that I could control my drinking. The incorporation of these new ideas coupled with the action-oriented program of AA started me down a path of re-creating my life's narrative and re-constructing my identity as an *alcoholic*...a sober alcoholic. My label as an alcoholic had been transformed as well, from a liability to a strength because I had created a new narrative and new meaning associated with the term alcoholic. I now know what it means to be an alcoholic.

One final thought about substances, identity and stigma in the treatment environment has to do with medications. Medications are also substances and like alcohol (and marijuana for the most part) are legal. Legality, though unimportant, often serves to distort reality. When discussing marijuana, say in a group therapy setting, denial seems to manifest in the statement, "It's legal." Prescribed medications often replace *illicit* substances as the client's primary coping mechanism. This is equally as harmful, in my opinion, in both dual and non-dual diagnosis populations. I have spoken with several physicians to confirm my suspicions that people build tolerance to most or all substances whether prescribed by a physician or purchased in a dark alley. What does that mean? It means that a person is going to need more medication to maintain the gains they have achieved by using said medication. In essence the same cycle of addiction becomes active only it is reinforced by the idea that it was prescribed by a doctor.

Of course, there are the cases where medication is absolutely necessary, but for those of the non-necessary class, who do not incorporate coping skills, they are destined for an eventual relapse as tolerance builds. This makes me wonder why the criteria of tolerance was removed from the most current edition of the DSM. I have met a few psychiatrists who actually engage in psychotherapy, but my experience in the treatment center realm has not confirmed the majority do. Many individuals manifest the same behaviors which have incapacitated their lives outside the treatment environment while they are in treatment, often stating, "I am waiting for my meds to kick in." This again becomes part of the identity. An identity that believes there will be no emotional distress in their lives if only they get the right amount or type of medication or drugs. What is forgotten is the lessons on how to "live life on life's terms" (also a slogan used in AA).

Considering the variety of topics previously discussed, we will move on to the discussion of how the 12-step process coincides with the various schools of psychotherapeutical thought. In an effort to create a work which is appealing and helpful to both mental health professionals and the general public, the discussions about therapeutic philosophies and intricacies remain at an intermediate level. For those with advanced knowledge of psychology and psychotherapy, the hope is that you will be able to homogenize information which you may find useful. For others, the hope is that you will find useful information to discuss with relevant people and/or find that this information sparks a curiosity which will lead to further exploration and learning. We will examine how narratives and identities are changed thorough cognitive and behavioral actions to help create satisfying lives and the relations between the two recovery models. In essence, we will travel down a two-lane highway arriving at a destination of being able to live life on life's terms yourself, or in helping others to do so.

The Psychodynamic Perspective

When discussing the psychodynamic school of thought, I am bringing into the fold the ideas of Freud, Jung, and attachment theory, as well as some of the new neurobiological findings discussed by Siegel and the like. More evidence is pouring in to support the actual "curing" of alcoholism and drug addiction through means such as a new attachment experience. In speaking with therapists who are object relations oriented, it seems these ideas spring forth with the hope of disputing the 12-step concept of… only through abstinence can one remain sober. That a person who has suffered with and in addiction can one day drink or use like the proverbial "gentleman." This may be true for a small number of such "problem drinkers," however AA and other 12-step societies may question whether a person like that is truly addicted. This person may fit the category of a heavy drinker or user versus the previously discussed, "true alcoholic" who qualifies as such, evidenced by their inability to stop once having started to drink or use. That is to say… stay stopped.

As anyone who can relate to the previous description will understand, staying stopped is the crux of the problem. Often alcoholics and addicts will stop for a day or two or even longer (I promised myself to stay sober a year to prove that I was not an alcoholic… I made it 11 months and 3 weeks telling myself, "11 months and 3 weeks *was* a year), often with

The Psychology of the 12 Steps

the intent to "regroup" or reset themselves for more drinking and using. More often this action serves to reinforce the mistaken belief that the person *can* quit whenever they want. There are times when this "true" alcoholic/addict is solemnly devoted to making it work, that is "quitting forever", but they find themselves quickly in the same spot or worse off than before. AA case experience has shown that one's relapse starts not where the last bender ended, but where it would have started had there been no abstinence at all; that indicates progression while not ingesting alcohol.

Provided that the great obsession of every abnormal drinker is to drink like a normal drinker (Alcoholics Anonymous, 2001). Drinking, when combined with the pain and misery it affords the alcoholic, I find it difficult to comprehend why someone, ergo a "healthcare" professional would encourage moderation in the face of its many failures. Despite the "Big Book's" assertion to step over to the nearest barroom and try some controlled drinking experiments, if one is not sure they are an alcoholic, it seems egotistical to me that pride would fuel the dangerous experiment of encouraging the first drink; but maybe I am projecting. Especially when the answer to the problem for millions looks them square in the eye. At times I wonder if we therapists are not so unlike those, we seek to aid… too smart for our own damn good.

When one reads the previously mentioned volumes related to AA's history, you will find that Bill Wilson was quite an entrepreneur and promoter. Additionally, he was quite intelligent, driven and influential. Given that understanding, it seems hardly an accident that the psychological concepts presented in the AA "Big Book" are those of the most influential psychological minds of the time, Freud, Jung and Adler. A contributing factor in Bill finding his sobriety and a solution to his alcoholism was through the influence of a lifelong friend and alcoholic. This man went to Dr. Carl Jung for treatment in Europe (Alcoholics Anonymous 2001). To reiterate, the psychodynamic school of thought is largely evident in the book and program of Alcoholics Anonymous.

Let us begin with Freud. A major concept in AA or 12-step recovery is the idea of ego. More so, one's ego run wild. A common "program" description of the basic personality of an alcoholic is that of an egomaniac with no self-esteem, as is asserted in meetings. Although this is not in the "Big Book" verbatim, it is a common narrative which has taken hold and been effective in helping those in early recovery achieve a sense of humility.

Hypothetically, the alcoholic strives or is driven to overcompensate for the lack of esteem and ego in such a selfish and self-seeking manner that most of their interpersonal relationships suffer as a result. The "Big Book" speaks of stepping on the toes of our peers and being surprised when they retaliate. This may be representative of an intra-psychic conflict which tears at the individual. They seek and seek and seek being driven by the id. They accumulate. But often the amount or the method they use to accumulate may be creating conflict between the id and the superego. Additionally, Alcohol and drugs may simply serve as a way of alleviating the tension, also known as anxiety of this internal conflict or the conflict between ego and self-esteem.

To further illustrate, the accumulated stuff creates an illusion of worthiness, self-esteem and ego in the consciousness. However unconsciously, the individual may be at odds with themselves, as mentioned above, which increases anxiety and psychic discomfort. The alcohol or drugs tends to relieve this and associated stress, and a pattern or cycle of maladaptive functioning is manifested. Of course, this may not be an exact scenario for all who suffer from chemical dependency, as traumatic experience and/or neglect are also quite common experiences. Nonetheless, I can tell you from my interactions with hundreds that it resonates with many. I dare say the majority rather than many. As such, it becomes a key rallying point for recovery. The trick of course is being able to mobilize or lower the defenses enough to allow for this realization if it is there. Regardless as to the extent which this may be valid in an individual, one thing is true. The resulting anxiety or fear however it was developed, creates the psychic distress. Alcohol and drugs relieve that distress. It works… for a while anyways.

The true concept of ego regarding the "Big Book" is kept simple, as is in line with one of the key principles of 12-step recovery… "Keep it Simple." The three entities of Freud's concept of mind, id, superego and ego seem combined in this regard and the idea of the mind is more comprehensively viewed as the whole self in 12-step recovery.

Keeping it simple essentially means not overthinking situations, especially the situations which usually nudge individuals to the doors of 12-step societies. Nonetheless, ideas such as one's instincts having gone awry, and being driven by a hundred forms of fear (or anxiety if you are Freud) are discussed in AA's "Big Book." The emphasis on not overthinking may serve to lessen the person's defensiveness making them more able to have the unconscious become conscious. The "ah ha" (personal insight) moment is constantly spoken of both in and out of group settings. These moments eventually become sought out phenomena, again serving to lower the individual's defensive tendencies, providing for an even more robust recovery.

Carl Jung's influence can also be seen, as related to the issue of spirituality. Spirituality seemed a key context of Jungian psychotherapy and a good friend of Bill's named Rowen H. was treated by Jung, as mentioned. Though not named in the "Big Book," he was described as an "American businessman of ability, good sense and high character (Alcoholics Anonymous, 2001. Pp. 26)." The paragraph also illustrates his difficulties in attaining sobriety. Following a certain treatment period with Jung, Rowen described his mental state and beliefs in a way which indicated he was confident in his recovery. Nonetheless, he was at another bottom because of his drinking shortly thereafter. He returned to Europe seeking out that which was baffling him. There he asked for the truth about his condition. Jung revealed, that in his opinion, Rowen's chances for recovery were hopeless. He described Rowen as a chronic alcoholic and the great doctor had never seen a single recovery in a person who possessed that state of mind.

Nonetheless, Rowen was told by Dr. Jung that there were cases which he had read about in which people have had "vital spiritual experiences (Alcoholics Anonymous, 2001. Pp.27)." Jung described these experiences as entire upheavals of personal convictions, beliefs and lifelong ideas in which these convictions were rearranged and became new. Jung reported that he had been attempting to promote this change in Rowen during their therapy sessions (Alcoholics Anonymous, 2001).

As it was, Rowen H found it useful to share the information he had learned with others in an effort to improve his spiritual connection, though it is not covered in detail in the "Big Book," but is in other AA literature. At one point he helped a mutual friend of his and Bill's named Ebby T. Rowen had convinced a judge to release Ebby into his care as part of his own recovery from alcoholism. This event is written of in "Bill's Story (Alcoholics Anonymous, 2001. Pp. 1-16)."

It was Ebby T. who approached Bill, as recorded in the cited pages of the text. In this story, Ebby told Bill that he found the answer to his alcoholism in God and religion. Bill scoffed with contempt. Bill thought to himself following Ebby's admission, "So that was it- last summer an alcoholic crackpot; now I suspected, a little cracked about religion (Alcoholics Anonymous, 2001. Pp. 9)." This is where the Oxford Group meetings in New York City were introduced to Bill via Ebby T. As is recorded in certain AA literature, such as "Pass it on" and "Alcoholics Anonymous Come of Age," Bill found some periods of relief from his alcoholism, but more importantly began to form the basic ideas that would eventually develop into the program of AA.

An entire upheaval of one's convictions, beliefs, and lifelong ideas, as Jung stated, form the basis of a new perspective and new motivation for living. This is the spiritual experience which is spoken of in AA's Big Book. This is also the point of contention which is difficult for many newcomers to the fellowship to maneuver through, as it requires the deconstructing of many defenses and mistaken beliefs. This leaves the newly sober individual distressed and often resistant. Nonetheless, AA promises the doorway to spirituality is much wider to walk through than it appears to the closed mind. I am not sure where, if anywhere the school of psychological thought lies on this, but I do admit that most treatment centers (all that I have worked in at least) provide space for the incorporation of the 12-step model and concepts. Additionally, I found a class in my Doctoral studies to be of particular interest and relevance. It was called Spirituality and Psychotherapy.

Many alcoholics and addicts, or people in general for that matter have a hard time with God. I do not know if it is bias or what, but it seems that this point of conflict is especially acute with the substance abuser. Whether it is a tempting of fate, an act of defiance or simply the inability to relinquish the illusion of control, it is difficult to say. However, what is apparent is the idea, or often more commonly, the contesting of the idea of God and religion in the experience of the addicted. Although Adler merited an entire chapter, a person's coming to terms with or without spirituality is a vital life task, which if not completed is believed to be a contributor to a person's non-useful behaviors, speaking in Adlerian terms.

Attachment Theory is a concept discovered through the

psychodynamic perspective which suggests that developmental and early childhood experiences, as related to our caregivers, shape our reactions to life's situations and relationships. Advances in neurobiological research indicate that these experiences form our synaptic connections, ultimately shaping the functioning of the mind (Siegel, 2012). Basically, one's personality or disposition is influenced or determined by the relationship one has with one's caregivers in the developmental years of life. This emerging evidence from the field of neurobiology strongly supports many of the concepts of personality psychology and psychodynamic perspectives which were difficult to find support for in the past. Researchers such as Dan Siegel have linked findings in attachment dynamics to a significant number of those identifying with alcoholism, addiction, and other mental health and behavioral disorders. Although stopping short of declaring that unfavorable attachments in childhood equate to mental health problems, such as substance addiction, Sigel does illustrate the relationship.

As a comprehensive review of attachment theory, and subsequently object relations theory is somewhat outside the scope of this book, it is, safe to say that my experience in AA recovery is riddled with stories of insecure and disorganized attachments, rather than secure attachments. But that is not to say individuals who experienced secure attachments do not exist in the program, which again brings to the forefront the theory of an allergy in the physiological realm.

Bill wrote in the AA text that he believed that there was a point where an alcoholic could have halted their drinking and remained a social imbiber. Yet, we had crossed that threshold into uncontrolled drinking (Alcoholics Anonymous, 2001). Maybe this is the case with the people who had what is described as secure attachments. It seems that it could be possible that these securely attached individuals simply enjoyed drinking and socializing so much the never reached and crossed the obscure line into dependence, thus triggering the phenomenon of craving. Whereas, in other cases of those who experienced secure attachments, these individuals did not find it necessary or were averse to the idea of drinking; let alone using more socially unacceptable substances, thus they never approached the line. Of course, one cannot forget that alcohol and substance (legal or not) use is higher in populations suffering from mental health issues, whether that use be described or cataloged as disordered, dependent or an addiction. That also includes securely and insecurely attached individuals.

Siegel reviews prominent research findings related to neural pathway development related to how one's caregivers raise and nurture the person in early childhood. These findings show long term changes in the brains ability to produce serotonin when attachment experiences are less than favorable. These changes in the brain lead to a vulnerability to anxiety, which medication (legal and socially acceptable substances) alleviates… Alleviates for a time that is. Often these individuals become dependent on these medications, at times escalating to the point of disordered use. Also, the eventuality of tolerance intercedes, and they again cannot function or cope despite use of the medication. Siegel confirms this dependence by discussing the fact that behavioral problems return following the cessation of a pharmacological regiment. Additionally, this then indicates how neural pathway development shapes brain functions related to emotional regulation, social relationships, and behavior in general (Siegel, 2012.)

When this is discussed in therapy sessions, defensiveness often manifests in the accusation that I am anti-medication, to which I assure these patients that I am simply anti-dependence, whatever the substance may be; legal or illicit. This is my belief set, of course. AA does not necessarily have an opinion on the use of pharmaceuticals outside the assertion that if a person receives a prescription from a doctor and adheres to the stated parameters, there is no issue. What is more, the "Big Book" encourages the use of other professionals to assist with issues outside of AA's single purpose. This purpose, broadly stated, is to help others recover from alcoholism (Alcoholics Anonymous, 2001)

Another finding in neuroscience is related to brain or neural plasticity. Neural plasticity refers to the brain's ability to "re-wire" itself. More specifically, the brain can restructure the established neural pathways. When these pathways are established through adverse attachments, emerging evidence suggests maladaptive functioning in the areas of emotional regulation, social relationships, and behavior in general follows. This phenomenon may explain a belief held by many I have heard speak in meetings; that they have always felt awkward, insecure, and/or detached from society.

Siegel reveals that these pathways re-wire themselves through new actions and new experiences (Siegel, 2012). This becomes the crux of recovery, both in dual and non-dual diagnosis populations, largely due to the internal dialogues these individuals employ as related to their experienced anxiety. Many of these individuals seek change, but when taking a new action is suggested or prescribed, they remain stagnant, employing any number of excuses or defenses. These individuals do nothing new and wonder why nothing in their lives or minds change. The basic formula is-

1) Employ a new action/engage in a new behavior, + 2) Have a new experience, = 3) Re-wiring of neural pathways which leads to new perspectives and more new behavior.

Of course, it is not that simple because the new experience may result in unexpected consequences whether desired or not. If left to the afflicted person's decision-making process, the choices made may be enacted out of distorted thinking or mistaken beliefs, which is likely to promote or prolong maladaptive functioning. Therefore, speaking of course in terms of the ideal dynamic, people are likely to benefit from working with a therapist. Consequently, this is also why people who go to 12-step societies for recovery will likely benefit from working with a sponsor.

In terms of attachment theory, object-relations oriented therapists whom I have spoken with attempt to recreate a healthy attachment as a key parameter of treatment. Empathy and reflection tend to be the curative mechanism. In the 12-step societies, the sponsor becomes the mechanism of a new and different attachment experience. The newly sober individual is encouraged, sometimes more strongly than others to take new actions and engage in new behaviors. Often the idea or intent towards taking these actions are residing in the preconscious mind. Yet, it is these very intentions that are likely creating a lot of anxiety in the person and they remain immobile using defenses in an unproductive way. However, when the action is taken, an experience is had, which is often discussed with the sponsor or shared about in a meeting. Often those who have more sober time and experience discuss these new experiences with the individual who has just taken this step towards change and is encouraged and supported. These new experiences, as discussed begin to activate the neural plasticity and change pathways and the person's thinking begins to change. Anxiety about taking uncomfortable actions or behaviors is reduced. A helpful slogan/platitude I learned in my AA recovery which illustrates this idea is, "You have to learn to be comfortable being uncomfortable." I like to use this concept with the people I work with today when anxiety is a presenting problem. Again, this is a process which takes time, as does effective psychotherapy.

This explanation is a summary of that process which is better described as a rollercoaster versus an ascent up a hill. Nonetheless, this experience becomes the mechanism of alleviating the emotional and behavioral distresses which have been the cause of many anxieties and distortions in the minds of the alcoholic or addict. Additionally, trust also begins to build via the new attachment experience and the person begins to feel a part of, rather than apart from the larger society.

Paul V.Z. Psy. D.

I remember a member who had accumulated over 40 years of sobriety solidify this assertion by discussing the phenomena with me after I shared in a meeting that I felt like I was part of the world again in my early sobriety.

Adlerian Psychotherapy

Alfred Adler is, in my opinion, ***the*** most underappreciated figure in psychology, at least in "pop" psychology. Although it is beyond the scope of this book, Adler was, to a certain extent, responsible for nearly all the major psychological philosophies employed in clinical psychotherapy today. In my first class of graduate studies, we were informed that we were to choose a theoretical orientation from which to view all our conceptualizations throughout our studies and training. Which would I choose? Freud is the grandfather. Jungian psychology seems so mystical and intriguing. The professor, having learned of my recovery history, or possibly just surmising it from my language, suggested Adlerian style to me. "Who the hell is Alfred Adler" I thought to myself. I had a bachelor's in psychology, and I did not really recognize the name. So, I followed the principle which had been instilled in me through the 12-step program and I simply took the next indicated step and followed the suggestion of another person (not just any person, of course, but a credible person).

I discussed earlier how Bill Wilson was no fool, but a shrewd promoter and businessman. He was also pragmatic and guided by the belief that he could only stay sober by sharing his experience with another alcoholic to help that person achieve sobriety. As such, it seems likely that he understood some type of fellowship was needed. Bill was also motivated not only by that entrepreneurial spirit, but also by the spirit of service and desire to help as many people as possible recover from their hopeless state of mind and body. As such, I hypothesized that he would likely include the top psychological theories of the day in a book he was writing about recovery from alcoholism; a disorder or disease for which a person in those days would be shut away in an asylum.

Whether it was of Bill's plan or the plan of Bill's higher power, as many in the program believe the formation of AA to be divine, it is apparent that the influences of the three, who are considered the fathers to modern clinical psychology, can be seen in the writings of AA's "Big Book." Freud and Jung were spoken of previously. Now for what is apparently Adler's influence.

For Alfred Adler, a key premise of his philosophy, which was also one of his therapeutic mediums, was the idea of building social interest or fellowship and connection with his fellow humans. Adler believed that through people and in building relationships with people, one becomes more inclined to achieve and is pulled toward their goals and towards the goal self-completion.

This idea of building social interest, holds true in the spirit of service espoused in the rooms of 12-step recovery. The concept of social interest or fellowship is also apparent in the common belief of AA that *I* cannot recover alone, but **WE** can recover together. The concept of social interest, or rather the contrary, also resonates in the idea delivered in the AA text that the alcoholic behaves in selfish, self-seeking, and self-centered ways. Both AA and Adler discuss this idea in their writings. The likely extent, etiology, and awareness of said self-focused behavior was discussed in the previous chapter, as Adler's Individual Psychology is also a psychodynamic approach. This is an essential area of focus undertaken in the 4th step which deconstructs the person's life in terms of their behavior and motivation behind those behaviors. This again is in line with Adler's belief that all behavior is goal oriented. Additionally, the social interest building activities encouraged in the 12-step societies are considered useful behaviors, in Adlerian terms.

Social interest is also a key component to the 12-step philosophy, as is evident in several of their slogans. "We care" and "Together We Can" to illustrate just a few. The actual mechanism or dynamic of building social interest is evident in the area of service commitments. A service commitment is where a member *commits* to employ various vital meeting functions. For instance, making coffee, serving as a secretary or treasurer, or distributing literature to name just a few. Some of the more vital jobs have certain requirements, in terms of sober time, but creative sponsors find picking up cigarette butts or simply setting up or putting away the chairs and tables serve as ways to get their newly sober prospects involved in building social interest, as well as increasing visibility with group members.

The levels, lengths and types of commitments generally fall in line with the amount of sober time, as mentioned. However new members are often encouraged to greet people at the door (something I prescribe to confront a person's social anxiety) to more intricate commitments on service boards at the macro & meso levels of the organization. New members are encouraged to get commitments at meetings, with the expressed purpose of "getting out of yourself (the opposite of being selfish, self-centered and self-seeking)," "being of service," or "giving back what was given to you (altruism)."

At the fundamental level, social interest is achieved. Often what happens is that the new person's social network expands because members with more sober time engage with these individuals and eventually become acquainted with them. Many of these older (speaking of sober time and sometimes chronologically) form relationships with the newcomer in both mentorship and sometimes attachment capacities. As this effect snowballs, the newly sober alcoholic/addict starts to run into members around town and begins to feel less like they are the only one who understands what they are going through. Hence, normalizing the problem and likely alleviating much self-imposed stigma. The action of mentoring is key in this dynamic, as those who have achieved and maintained sobriety understand the importance of getting new people involved in the 12-step society, as they were instructed when they were new. It would seem they understand the importance of building social interest, even if they do not know who Alfred Adler is.

Another of Adler's premises is the idea of a person's innate feeling of inferiority. More aptly described this feeling is related to the idea of self-completion or superiority, as Adler put it. Human children versus most other creatures in the animal kingdom, have an extended period of dependence upon their caregiver's. This reality is what fueled Adler's assertion of an innate feeling of inferiority. As such the person is pulled by the goal of life task completion which in turn fulfills the quest for superiority over life's challenges (not superiority over other beings).

For humans, the time period of parental and social dependence is years to decades. In today's world, it seems that the period of parental dependence is increasing even more, which may indicate why there also seems to be a spike in alcoholism, addiction, and psychopathology. From a developmental perspective, it is the child's interpretation of the life task experience which eventually leads to useful or useless behavior. However, complications can arise as the parental experience is interpreted through the child's mind, which is yet capable of complex thought. The child's mind does not conceptualize abstractly, and often leads to the development of mistaken beliefs (Adler, 1927) which dominate perception. This interpretation is what leads to inferiority feelings which a person may or may not be aware. Essentially, Adler believed that inferiority feelings were simply a part of the human experience, as we are all in life situations which we would like to improve. As such, the idea of an inferiority complex has become associated with Adler. Though it is likely that he is not the person who coined the phrase. (Ansbacher & Ansbacher, 1956).

Adler wrote that the abnormal feeling of inferiority has been given the name "inferiority complex," but that he questioned the accuracy of a description of inferiority *feelings* as a complex. He questioned the accuracy, as he described the inferiority feeling as permeating the entire personality. Additionally, he indicated that having inferiority feelings was less important than "it's degree and expression (Adler, 1927)." The feeling of inferiority in and of itself is believed to be a motivating factor towards a healthy and satisfying life, in terms of the goals a person wishes to achieve. It is when a person becomes overwhelmed by these feelings and a sense of inadequacy prevails, does it become problematic which is essentially the "complex" state. The "complex" is exacerbated when it immobilizes, in the way of depression, and an individual's lack of engagement in useful behaviors. Hence, useful behaviors are used overcome the conditions that are creating the inferiority feelings (Ansbacher & Ansbacher, 1956).

What is being suggested is that the way in which a person attempts to cope with these feelings is what leads to the distinction as to whether they are adaptive or maladaptive coping styles. The healthier approach, in Adler's opinion was in seeking socially useful ways of achieving these strivings for self-completion. On the other hand, Adler stated that non-useful attempts to alleviate inferiority feelings, fueled by discouragement, could be evidenced by withdrawing from social interests and engaging in antisocial behavior. Additionally, these attempts often manifested in the development of a superiority complex, which is a maladaptive compensation for one's feeling of inferiority, as opposed to a healthy feeling of superiority, as related to creating a useful socially focused life (Ansbacher & Ansbacher, 1956).

This brings us to the concept of "style of life" or "lifestyle convictions." As all people have feelings of inferiority, the goal of each person is to strive for superiority in the sense of self-completion or the overcoming of life's problems. This is a part of the lifestyle conviction. Adler wrote much in connection with a person's style of life and it is noted that his later writings seemed to differentiate or expand on his original concept. Nonetheless, it is generally accepted that a person's style of life is comprised of the goal, the person's opinion of themselves and the world, and their unique way of striving for that goal in different situations (Ansbacher & Ansbacher, 1956). Also included in Neo-Adlerian conceptualizations of a person's lifestyle are the ideas concerning personal ethical convictions and one's personality traits (Corsini, 2011).

For the alcoholic and addict, it seems their difficulties stem from a misguided lifestyle conviction, largely energized by their mistaken beliefs and strivings for their fictional goal. Adler surmised their attempts thusly, "Alcoholics seek relief from their problems… satisfied from the relief that comes from a bottle (Adler, 1927. Pp. 132)." I argue that this is true to a significant extent, as related to lifestyle, mainly in the sense of self-concept or how the alcoholic/addict views themselves and the world in which they live.

A powerful insight that was thrust into my consciousness at the point of being beaten (by alcohol) into a state of reasonableness was my goal. The work goal specifically; where I was *supposed* to be or planned to be versus where I was. My work goal was more in line with what I thought others would want, than with what I genuinely wanted and as such was what is known as the fictional goal. This presented an incongruence, which without the veil of alcohol became acutely painful. This painful discomfort coupled with limited choices, as well as a few *coincidental* encounters put me on the road to recovery. What I am suggesting, as is in line with Adlerian concepts, is the idea of living congruently. Living congruently, meaning how one views themselves versus *knowing* that view is accurate. Alcohol and other substances tend to cloud that view by promoting the fictional goal which activates non-useful behaviors to cope with feelings of inauthenticity, thus exacerbating inferiority feelings. As mentioned earlier, an idea that resonates with many alcoholics and addicts is the idea of having an exaggerated ego, coupled with no self-esteem. This seems accurate when placed into the paradigm of inferiority feelings, coping with them, and the superiority complex.

Adler professed living, living usefully that is, takes courage (Adler, 1927). The moniker "liquid courage" may indicate a certain truth in the functionality of alcohol and other substances in an inauthentic life. Another helpful platitude commonly espoused in the rooms of 12-step recovery is that alcohol and drugs were the solution (lifestyle conviction) in the person's life, rather than the problem. That solution was for the actual problem of an inability to live life on life's terms or as Adler would put it, living with courage. However, given the dismissed (in the DSM-V) concepts of tolerance and progression, the solution eventually became the problem. This process seems to also be true about medications given to treat mental health symptoms according to Siegel's research findings discussed in the previous chapter. The medication (drug), also known as a substance (prescribed or not), eventually loses efficacy due to tolerance. As such, when there is no learning, as far as useful and productive behaviors is concerned, the symptoms return, and a higher dose or stronger medication is needed to alleviate the symptom; hence, progression. I argue that the true symptom, for either the alcoholic/addict or the mentally ill (moderately afflicted) is being unable to live life on life's terms.

When considering Adler's philosophical and therapeutic paradigm, one cannot leave out the idea of completing prescribed life tasks to achieve superiority. For those unfamiliar with the concept, it is a benevolent superiority, not an oppressive type. In this regard, superiority can be summed up in terms of the superiority one feels having achieved and or completed personal and societal developmental markers. It is a superiority over self, as related to self-completion and in overcoming life situations (Adler, 1927).

The way in which an individual achieves this superiority is by the completion of life tasks combining and contributing to the previously described feelings of authenticity. A general categorization of the life tasks areas includes work/career, belonging/love/sex, and building social interest which are directly addressed by Adler, and are more clearly defined in his writings (Adler, 1927). Adlerian scholars indicate two other life tasks he alluded to in his work as being able to deal/cope with one's self, and lastly, to be able to deal/cope with the concept of spirituality (Ansbacher & Ansbacher, 1956). Adler believed that by achieving these tasks, one attains a feeling of completion, also known in this case as a feeling of superiority, as opposed to the detrimental superiority *complex* which is an unhelpful overcompensation technique. This superiority over life's challenges is what Adler believed to the true goal versus the fictional goal, in terms of one's lifestyle convictions. It is the striving for the fictional goal, in a non-useful manner which leads to problematic symptomology, distress, and unproductive behavior. Adler lends credence to my previously stated experience, that alcoholics and addicts are seeking a shortcut; an easier, softer way. He states, "In the neurosis one will always find... increased inferiority feeling... the patient constantly seeks an easier way (with regards to society, occupation, sexuality) (Ansbacher & Ansbacher, 1956. Pp. 255)," thus becoming the fictional goal.

From this perspective, the essential life tasks to be completed are inherent to 12-step living. To begin, the first task related to work, and career is a springboard to recovery. The unconditional love and charity provided to newcomers by sponsors in the programs is done so with only the spirit of service to others in mind, ideally speaking, of course. Members often prudently jest, in a manner intended to raise awareness in newcomers, that AA is not the hot bed of mental health. Nonetheless, the only "catch" is cloaked in the hope that the newcomer who was given said charity recovers and carries that spirit to the next individual they may sponsor. In order to make that happen, one usually needs to get a job. Hence, work, employment or career is encouraged, if not demanded by the sponsor. Many case studies abound illustrating returns to college programs which were abandoned due to drinking or drugging. Others return to previously held jobs or get entry level jobs (known as "get well" jobs) and flourish; while yet others embark on new careers entirely, as eventually came to pass in my case.

Next, is the life task of love and belonging. It is often heard in the rooms of AA… for that matter in therapy rooms as well, that people feel like they do not belong (as a part of society). This sentiment can also be articulated as feeling unloved or worthless. Inherently, 12-step programs provide a sheltering safe harbor for people who are in this boat. AA welcomes the homeless, the friendless, the moneyless, and many more while helping them get back on their feet. The embodiment of this concept is expressed in the common AA motto, "let us love you until you can love yourself." To a greater or lesser degree this motto is transformed into action apparent in many 12-step members as they selflessly engage in a truly altruistic existence both in and out of AA.

Lastly, the concept of building social interest is so fundamental to Adler's philosophy that it has been discussed earlier. The level of engagement with other's socially and altruistically is one of the ways Adler believed a person's mental health could be assessed. According to him, people who are dominated by an inferiority complex and striving for a fictional goal tend to behave in an anti-social manner, such as withdrawing from or manipulating others. The superiority complex manifests as part of this non-useful side of social interest (Adler, 1927). Fortunately, the previously noted way in which the 12-step societies address and engage in the building of social interest is what Adler would term as useful, thus helping it members to complete life tasks and create a more satisfying life.

Spirituality and religion, rather coming to terms with or learning to cope with spirituality and religion is also a subject which many include in the realm of life tasks. As I surmised earlier, this is an issue that though experienced by most people, seems especially apparent with alcoholics and addicts. One is likely to wonder if this is not one of the essential bases of anxiety that the person is trying to escape through the use or misuse of substances. It appears Adler had some thoughts on the matter. "The fact that an increasingly large portions of mankind resists religion does not arise from the essential nature of religion. This resistance rather originates from the contradictions which have resulted between the action of the power apparatus of the religions and their essential nature, and probably also from the not infrequent abuses of religion (Ansbacher & Ansbacher, 1956. Pp. 462)." I have experienced people discussing these frustrations in meeting shares, in the parking lot after the meeting, and during post meeting coffee gatherings. Of course, though a Freudian concept, displacement may be occurring, as one tries to avoid the discomfort of their own hypocrisy… but I digress.

Adler spoke of the "essential nature of religion" which I argue is what most mean when they say, "I am spiritual, not religious." It seems this is a way to believe in God or a Higher Power without condoning or aligning oneself with the past and recent revelations concerning the activities in Christian institutions, both denominational and non, as well as the tyrannical and bloody history of most religions trying to prove that theirs is the one true God.

Bill Wilson wrote in the text "Alcoholics Anonymous" that he believed that almost everybody had the fundamental idea of God within them. Adler jousted philosophically with a well-known Protestant minister of the time regarding the nature of guidance and psychotherapy from both perspectives; religious and spiritual. What was revealed was the difference in how one viewed God. Adler viewed God as a concept or an idea, whereas the minister viewed God as an absolute reality (Ansbacher & Ansbacher, 1956). It is difficult to say where Bill stood in this regard, however it does seem apparent that he believed that a Higher Power is fundamental in attaining and maintaining effective sobriety. This in essence seems to sum up the concept of the life task related to learning to deal or cope with God or a higher power.

Adler's *idea* of God is associated with perfection, greatness and superiority (Adlerian superiority) and as such, he believed this to be a likely goal for many. He supported this in the assertion of man's self-stated quests to---follow God's call, walk with Him or be one with Him. What is more, he classified these as goals of striving. Strive goals are different from drive goals, as the latter are attributed to instinctual desires related to survival. As such, an individual chooses to adopt attitudes, thoughts and feelings as a result of *striving* to be more God like (Ansbacher & Ansbacher, 1956). Could it be, given the explanation of Adler's thoughts on how our experiences in early childhood manifest, that a mistaken conception of God is at the heart of spiritual/religious contention? I do not believe it to be unreasonable to assume such. I also assert that this fundamental mistaken belief could also lie at the heart of the unrealistic ventures at achieving perfection that is evident in the narratives of alcoholics, addicts and those with other mental health disorders.

So, it would appear that God is somewhat of a catch 22 that sets in motion a cycle of trying to attain an unattainable goal to relieve the anxiety of the individual's inferiority feeling. However, not achieving the goal simply increases the feelings of inferiority at which a person may exert more energy trying to alleviate or develop a superiority (God) complex. Referring to the concept that alcoholics and addicts are selfish, self-seeking and self-centered, it seems that the formation and display of this attitude is not that surprising or unexpected within the expressed paradigm of spirituality. Additionally, though I only speak from experience (not empirically), working with both substance dependent and the mentally ill, it seems that when one has and is connected with a higher power, anxiety is alleviated. This is evident in the individual's ability to let go of their desire to control everyone and everything. I think this could also be described as peace of mind and with peace of mind comes humility, in my opinion.

This is exactly the purpose in the exercise of developing humility as part of the 12-step program. The development of humility via useful actions rather than humiliation, that is. Although humiliation often is what brings an individual to the steps of the 12-step society's door and as such serves a purpose. Yet it is humility which eventually sets that person free. I remember hearing a useful moniker in this regard early in my sobriety and it helped remove the bitter taste I associated with my misunderstood idea of humility. It was that humility was not thinking less of yourself, but rather thinking of yourself less. That was a concept I could do business with, so to speak.

12-step societies utilize a variety of platitudes to instill this idea of becoming "right sized" or humble. Members discuss and share in meetings their journey on this desired road, continually reminding both themselves and others that this road is circular without a finish line meaning arrogance can and will return minus vigilance. Action oriented tasks such as commitments, helping others, sharing in meetings and asking someone to be their sponsor are some of the humility building behaviors that mentors suggest newcomers engage in. When the right amount of humility is achieved, one's relationship with both the idea of and the reality of God or a Higher Power is transformed. In my opinion, this process is reciprocating as one effects the other to varying degrees. Moreover, the amount of humility a person is displaying is directly related to his or her relationship with their Higher Power and vice versa. I am speaking to an ideal if you will. Of course, there are those who use God as a springboard of self-righteousness, but that is what would fall into Adler's concept of a superiority complex.

When this ideal is achieved, it is likely that person's perception, lifelong held ideas, beliefs and attitudes will have changed. This sounds like the vital spiritual experience Jung was speaking of in the previous chapter. Adler stated, "Now that man no longer see himself as the center of world events, he is satisfied… and is inclined to conceive it (God) as causally acting forces of nature (Ansbacher & Ansbacher, 1956. Pp. 460)." This statement is instrumental and again I am not certain if this is Bill's genius or that of a Divine plan. However, it is instrumental, as this idea serves to help individuals let go of some of the issues of delusional control over life. Again, platitudes or sayings are used to instill this idea. Platitudes such as, "that's God working in my life, let go and let God, or a higher power is doing for me, what I cannot do for myself." Many times, these quotes are expressed when speaking of coincidental events which have occurred in the person's life. Events such as, a job being offered without significant effort or speaking of a certain need to a confidant and someone who is casually walking by after a meeting overhearing the need is able to provide.

A final thought on God or a Higher Power, if you prefer, has to do with the individual's personal conception of the idea or the reality of God. I believe this to be especially important, at least it was in my own personal journey in recovery. Often people are restricted by the concepts of a Higher Power as presented and internalized in developmental stages of life. As previously hypothesized, this concept may have or more likely did form the basis of a mistaken belief about the true nature of spirituality. This mistaken belief then became the proverbial barb under the horse's saddle. Related constrictions and rigidity likely immobilize people in terms of changing that mistaken concept. However, Adler attests, "Each individual forms an image of the functioning and shape of the supreme being which differs from that of the next man by nuances of a thousand-fold variation (Ansbacher & Ansbacher, 1956. Pp. 460)." That statement speaks to the idea in 12-step recovery of "God, as you understand God." Bill discussed in the AA literature, how he feared the strict religious tenements of the Oxford Group could hinder a person's chances for recovery. This was also illustrated in Bill's initial response to Ebby, whom had a spiritual awakening and came to his home offering help. For that reason, being able to conceive one's own personal conception of a higher power appears to be liberating. Sponsors say things like, "you get to create a God that you can do business with." It is also helpful in motivating individuals who are adamant about the non-existence of God. The concept serves to help these people stay sober a while with the hopes of gaining some flexibility in thinking. In early sobriety, the idea of a Group Of Drunks (G.O.D.) could be used as a concept of a higher power in that the group has found a solution to their alcoholism and that the individual has not. Thus, constituting a power greater than that person.

There is something the "Big Book" calls a spiritual experience of an *educational* variety. In essence this translates into the idea that the result of taking the prescribed 12-steps eventually leads to the previously mentioned re-arranging of personal thoughts and beliefs. As a person progresses, they become less rigid in their thinking, essentially opening the mind and expanding their perspective. The individual becomes more adaptable or able to live life on life's terms without becoming reactionary. This makes me think of a Harvard professor I had for several classes in graduate and post graduate studies who defined good mental health as a person's ability to adapt to the situations that life presents. The most important thing, however, is to keep the person coming back and engaging in the program long enough to have a spiritual experience of an educational… or more aptly, a spiritual experience of the psychological variety.

Existentialism

Existentialism is less of an independent school of psychological thought or technical approach to psychotherapy/recovery as it is a representation of thinking and incorporating the tenants of the human experience. Some therapists believe that these ideas, have a place within any psychotherapeutical approach, as coming to terms with, or rather *not* coming to terms with these issues can be anxiety provoking. There is a story about Irvin Yalom, a prominent existentialist, who at one point in his life was taking a cooking class. Despite following the recipe precisely, he could not recreate the flavor of the dish such as did the instructor. One day he noticed that the teacher would hand off the dish to an assistant who proceeded to finish it in the oven. Yalom also noticed that at that time, the assistant would add his own touches in the form of additional seasonings before placing the dish in the oven. This prompted a revelation, according to Yalom, associated with therapeutic styles and effectiveness, as related to existentialism. Yalom conceptualize existential ideas and issues as extra "touches" that need to be included in psychotherapy to create a complex and tasty dish, if you will (Corsini, 2011).

As we have just finished with a discussion of Adler's Individual Psychology approach. It is important to note this too was an influence in modern psychotherapy that can be attributed to the man. Adler attested his belief that life, in essence, had no meaning. As such, it was the responsibility of the individual to create or construct meaning in an otherwise meaningless existence.

The striving for meaning essentially would lead to purposeful actions that would move the person in achieving purposeful goals (Corsini, 2011). However, if mistaken beliefs related to these ideas influenced this goal directed movement, the results would be incongruent or inauthentic, thus leading to more distress and anxiety (Ansbacher & Ansbacher, 1956).

Existentially oriented therapists view people as meaning making beings who are influenced by both experience and self-reflection. What is more, our knowledge of our own mortality becomes the catalyst with which we strive to have a meaningful and purposeful life. Our mortality fuels questions related to whom a person is, why a person is and whether that person matters. These and other existentially influenced self-reflections, such as choice, responsibility, and purpose in life form what Yalom called a person's ultimate concerns. The ultimate concerns include freedom, isolation, meaning, and death (Corsini, 2011). As far as the alcoholic, addict and 12-step philosophy of recovery is concerned, existentialism is visibly important in achieving initial recovery and in maintaining recovery, as we shall see.

Corsini states that many diagnosable symptoms may simply be masked existential issues which all therapists should consider and be aware of. He argues the possibility that it is more comfortable for some therapists to simply adhere to the standardized procedures of a manualized approach whether that be of a medical or psychological in nature. The more helpful alternative, according to Corsini, is the therapist's genuine engagement with the individual, and helping them achieve the meaning in life they are searching for. In this regard, the 12-step program looks to the sponsor, whom of course in not a therapist and is no substitute for a good therapist. However, the sponsor does provide a genuine relationship with the recovering member, while making action-oriented suggestions that ultimately lead to addressing the ultimate concerns posed by Yalom and Existentialism, such as meaning in life.

Existential freedom differs from freedom in the political sense. Existential freedom is aligned with the constructionistic idea that we live in a directionless universe and existence. Hence, we are ultimately in charge of creating our own lives. As Adler proposed, life is meaningless unless we take responsibility and choose to engage in behaviors that make it so. Existentialists believe that there is a certain fear or dread which is associated with this responsibility. Responsibility and choice are inextricably intertwined with this freedom and the psyche of an individual. Existentialists propose that there is a *knowing* associated with this ultimate responsibility for our experiences and that this *knowing* is burdensome or anxiety provoking. From an existential point of view, Corsini writes that the complement to responsibility is the will. He suggests that social science has moved towards removing this responsibility of choice away from the individual and attributing it to symptomology or pathology, to which I do not necessarily disagree.

However, I would likely argue that it is the medical model which is doing this more than social sciences. Nonetheless, the removal of this responsibility essentially promotes inauthentic living which the person recognizes at some existential level, thus creating more discomfort than it removes. He continues with a suggestion that some of the goals of existentially oriented psychotherapy include increasing freedom as related to choice and responsibility, freedom from non-useful habits, freedom from the maladaptive effects of self-defeating beliefs and ultimately embracing existential freedom.

Interestingly, from the 12-step perspective the will of the alcoholic or addict is something of a conundrum and is a key facet in the troubles they have created for themselves. The AA "Big Book" describes a key characteristic, rather character defect of the sufferer as a person whose self-will has run riot. What this means, in my experience is that the alcoholic/addict's essential motivations are misguided and is the factor behind the discourse in that person's existence. "So, our troubles we think, are basically of our own making. They arise out of ourselves, and the alcoholic is an extreme example of self-will run riot, though he usually doesn't think so (Alcoholics Anonymous, 2004. Pp. 62)." This excerpt, as well as other examples in the "Big Book" allude to the defenses which Corsini suggests are created as a result of the discomfort associated with living inauthentically.

The "Big Book" discusses how the lives of alcoholics are dichotomies in the way the alcoholic presents themselves to the world or how they wish to be perceived versus how they really are. This is essentially the inauthenticity spoken of previously. This dichotomy essentially leads to more discomfort and increased drinking or using to alleviate the discomfort. This is the rudimentary addiction cycle. In addition, it also leads to the activation and usage of some of the more common defenses in the psychotherapeutic lexicon, such as denial, avoidance, projection and displacement to name a just a few. From my experiences, as an active alcoholic, a recovering alcoholic, a sponsor and as a therapist, I can assure this to be true.

Displacement, also known as externalizing the problem seems to be especially rampant. This displacement is essentially skirting the existential responsibility of making useful choices in creating a satisfying life. The alcoholic and addict, whom is not on the path to recovery, is constantly blaming other people and circumstances for the continuation of their maladaptive behaviors. This displacement of blame or responsibility is also common in those with non-addiction related mental health issues. Until the individual begins to shift their perspective and accept responsibility for their choices, they will be on a path leading away from the creation of a spiritual experience (upheaval of one's belief systems) which facilitates the building of a new and satisfying existence, also known as recovery.

The subject of choice or the freedom to choose is an important issue in the realm of psychotherapy and is an admirable and desired treatment outcome for people. However, it is also a contentious area for mental health professionals who are not intricately familiar with the alcoholic and addict. It may be obscured by misinformation or misconception, in terms of removing the afflicted person's choices all together. This may also be why so many therapists desire an outcome in which a person with a substance use disorder discovers a way or learns how to drink or use in a controlled manner.

AA and 12-step societies on the other hand, view this inability to choose whether to imbibe moderately as the key factor in differentiating an alcoholic or addict from the casual, or even heavy/problematic drinker or user. Lack of choice, where drinking is concerned is what identifies *the real alcoholic* as illustrated in AA's "Big Book." This would hold true in the other 12-step programs as well. For example, the real cocaine addict or the real gambling addict. Once this person has taken the first snort or made the first bet, for whatever reason they have lost the choice until the manifestation of a sufficient amount of wreckage which creates so much emotional pain they again decide to abstain. Generally speaking, this is the "bottom" a person hits that activates the motivation to make an attempt to stop. Any type of great loss, for example a financial loss could constitute a bottom. However, any type of bottom it seems, tends to conclude in an emotional bottom (guilt and shame). The bottom motivates the afflicted to stop. Yet, as previously discussed, stopping is not the same as staying stopped.

Bill W. wrote extensively about choice, often relating it to the person's will. His experience as related to his drinking and with the people whom he worked with convinced him that the real alcoholic has lost his/her choice in the matter once having consumed the first drink and activating the previously mentioned allergy. However, once having stopped for a period of time, the individual could make choices, and take the appropriate actions that help him or her to remain sober as long as the person remained abstinent. It is the re-directing and re-focusing of the will which is paramount in this scenario.

Bill expressed in a letter the idea of our choice to accept certain helpful ideas. For instance, believing that one could not recover alone or in the practicing of the principles espoused in 12- step recovery programs to name just couple of helpful ideas. Furthermore, as most are resistant to the proposed principles and actions associated in maintaining them, there is most certainly a choice involved in becoming willing to try. One group I attended has an individual who relays his early experience of skepticism and relapse relating it to his unwillingness to accept what was offered to him. He would tell how his sponsor encouraged him to be willing. If that did not work, he was encouraged to willing to be willing and so on. Ultimately his resistance was lowered, and he commenced with recovery.

As the goal of psychology and psychotherapy is to help people become more adaptive or flexible, then it seems that the incorporation of beliefs and views which move people towards that ideal are paramount. An idea which has paralyzed alcoholics and addicts likely since the discovery of substance use is the idea that the afflicted can *choose* to drink or use *responsibly*. It appears simple to me now that I have maintained my sobriety for several years, that willingness and open-mindedness in this regard is the answer. However, I remember that I was as resistant as anyone to the idea of abstinence. This was likely because I did not have any other manner of coping with whatever it was, I was trying to cope with at the time, other than alcohol and drugs. Obviously, the answer is not that simple, and a person must construct an answer that works for them. However, I do not believe that the answer for the real alcoholic/addict is trying to instill a belief that one day with the right psychological formula, controlled drinking/using is possible.

Existential isolation is based on the premise that most people come into the world alone and leave this world alone. This differs from the common idea of isolation, as being separated from people or intrapersonal isolation, being separated from the self. Existentialists propose that people must manage a tension between desiring contact with others and the knowledge that we are essentially alone. Hence, this dilemma, much of the time is an unconscious struggle. Erich Fromm posits anxiety is the result of this isolation. Corsini describes existential isolation's difference as manifesting from the belief that there is an unbridgeable gap between the self and others. Yalom relates it to living an unobservable life, in terms of everyday activities. Existential isolation is also related to the idea that there is nobody watching over you and that in essence the universe does not care about the individual. Feeling apart from rather than a part of was discussed earlier as a common characteristic of alcoholics and addicts. It is likely that this feeling is related to existential isolation and is likely felt by all to some degree but may be felt more keenly in those who use substances to cope. From another perspective, it could be argued that codependents also keenly experience this isolation and is why these people are so absorbed in and by others.

From the 12-step recovery perspective, loneliness is addressed in meetings and is a likely focus of some sponsors. I have often heard individuals speak of feeling alone in a room full of people. Though I do not recall anyone referring to this as anything other than simple loneliness it is apparent that it is of the existential variety. The "12-Steps and 12-Traditions" (12 & 12) alludes to this existential isolation stating "Even before our drinking got bad, and people began to cut us off, nearly all of us suffered the feeling that we didn't quite belong (Alcoholics Anonymous, 2003. Pp. 57)." The 12-step recovery programs may help with the alleviation of such feelings as well. Existentially oriented psychotherapists posit that existential isolation does not go away completely, only that it can be managed. For that matter, the same can be said for anxiety. Hence, what is crucial is learning how to cope with and adapt to these feelings.

With that in mind, a likely avenue of reducing existential isolation and anxiety is the simple act of normalizing a person's feelings and experiences. This process was discussed earlier, as the person sharing in a meeting is often supported by others whom "can relate." Often people choose a sponsor because of something that person has shared in a meeting and that very thing could be existential isolation, further normalizing and lessening the experienced feelings. A sponsor may also provide solace related to the need for feeling watched over or cared about. The 12 & 12 discusses how meditation provides this experience for the recovering person, describing it as a medium for connecting with a Higher Power who watches over them and by providing the person with a sense of belonging.

Finding meaning in one's life is another point which Existentialists extoll as anxiety provoking and having the potential to throw a person into crisis; or at least create enough discomfort in a person leading them to adopt maladaptive thinking and actions. It is believed that people must find meaning in life, or a reason for living. What frustrates some is that there are none overtly indicated or given. An existential life task is that of finding a purpose in one's life. Adler described this roughly as the life task of building social interest. People present for therapy with existential meaning issues veiled behind statements of feeling useless, empty, and directionless. The therapist then is presented with the task of assisting such individuals in the finding and enacting of interests and actions which are likely to increase feelings of meaningfulness and purpose. Engagement in these interests essentially alleviates the discomfort by shifting a person's focus to something bigger than oneself to use a familiar cliché.

Although Existentialists posit that this feeling abounds in all people and is a condition which must be resolved, alcoholics, addicts, and those with acute mental health issues may be hypersensitive to the discomfort this creates. During my graduate and post graduate studies I found that the 12-step programs are structured in a way that promotes the resolution of existential meaninglessness. People come into the program with all their proverbial chips cashed in. That is to say, they are hopeless. By whatever means they engage in the repairing of their lives and existence. Following the direction of the program principles and a sponsor, they begin to start helping others. During this time, a host of compatriots, fellow recovering individuals grows around them, essentially building social interest or becoming a part of something bigger than themselves. They give back by becoming sponsors themselves, and engaging in service commitments, and a purpose in life is created. The individual has given meaning to their lives by simply engaging in their own recovery. Whether it is by design or happenstance that this dynamic manifests is a discussion for another time, yet it is evident nonetheless.

The condition of alcoholism is presented as a threefold disease of body, mind and spirit; physical, psychological, and spiritual. As such, each fold must be addressed and "treated." The initial time spent working with a sponsor is often focused on helping the newcomer not take the first drink which activates the allergy; physical. Next, the focus becomes that of managing the obsessional nature of the alcoholic or mental health conditions; psychological. These first two experiences are largely homogenized after the physical compulsion is alleviated in the first weeks. As recovery progresses, the program and sponsor encourage the newcomer to become involved in various types of service work in order to deal with the individual's spiritual malady, as it is described in the "Big Book." This spiritual malady, as I have hypothesized and presented to individuals I have worked with, is a malady of the human spirit, more so than a Godly spirit even though I believe they are intertwined. In my opinion, the human spirit, or will to live is greatly enhanced by having existential meaning or a purpose in one's life.

As the newcomer progresses in recovery, the focus begins to shift to the idea of "carrying the message," which is considered 12th step work, along with the other service type commitments. Just to note, effective sponsors are aware of this shift in focus in the newcomer and are alert to spot issues of codependency. If the focus becomes *too* much on others, in order to prevent a "switching of addictions," or increase of other non-productive behaviors the sponsor discusses and presents possible solutions or other helpful ideas. The purpose created by engaging in the 12- step program is one of helping others, or of being of service to others. Initially this begins at the level of involvement with other group members but is encouraged as a guiding principle to be carried into members' everyday lives. This principle is summed in the final phrase of the 12th step; "we tried to practice these principles in all our affairs."

Further along in the growth of the recovering individual, as related to the purpose of carrying the message, is that of becoming a sponsor themselves. Becoming a sponsor is a theme often spoken of with both anticipation and sometimes fear or nervousness. Nonetheless it is an undertaking most wish to engage in to support their desire to give back to the program which was so freely given to them. Not to mention it is heralded as a key factor in maintaining a robust recovery.

This becomes another intricate point in the creation of purpose in the person's life, thus leading to a greater feeling of existential meaning. Often as recovery progresses, or if an individual to sponsor has yet to materialize, the person becomes involved with commitments at higher levels, such as intergroup or general service board levels. These commitments are dedicated to the survival of AA (or whichever 12-step society they attend) in a sense, as they are responsible for communication between the individual groups and the greater entity of AA. The bottom line is that there are several ways to carry the message and be a part of something bigger than oneself in the 12-step societies, all of which aid in bringing a greater meaning to one's life. This purpose which is created through selfless involvement for others' benefit, and in being a part of something greater than oneself, is in my opinion, what leads to the healing of one's human spirit and is an innate part of the 12-step recovery programs.

To carry the message to other alcoholics who are still suffering... is the single purpose of Alcoholics Anonymous. This is one of the 12 traditions in the society and was forged out of the experience of an earlier group known as the Washingtonians. This group began having success using spiritual principles in the recovery of alcoholism and received public acknowledgment. Bill discovered that the reason for their eventual demise was because they began trying to expand their ideas and apply them to other social ills, thus diluting their message.

A criticism I have heard in the professional realm is related to this tradition of singleness of purpose. Clients in treatment centers do not understand why it is frowned upon to state that they are addicts in a closed AA meeting and thusly condemn the whole process which often leads to relapse. At that point, uniformed therapists cannot aid them in the processing of their emotions without the facts about why it is so, which is not helpful. As such and as both a clinician and individual in recovery, I present this information which I believe can be helpful in this matter. AA's rigidity in this matter is one of survival for AA and the millions which they have helped recover. AA as an entity does not want to follow in the footsteps of the Washingtonian group. Less rigid sponsors will jest, by stating something like, "Yeah... Bill didn't use drugs until page seven." Alluding to a section in "Bill's Story" which he states that he used sedatives to calm delirium tremens. Others not that in the *Doctor's Opinion* section of the book, Dr. Silkworth notes alcoholics as people addicted to alcohol. Nonetheless, AA tradition of singleness of purpose remains, for good reason. This is also why there are so many types of 12-Step programs, each has a single purpose or focus.

It is apparent that comorbidity of mental health, emotional and relationship problems are inherently evident in alcoholics and drug addicts. To me, that seems to be another reason that there are so many 12-step programs available to help suffering individuals. They are a helpful addition to therapy or vice versa. However, all have a singleness of purpose and in that spirit, it is customary to express that something outside that group purpose manifests as part of whatever the group focus is. For example, a statement may be constructed as, "In the midst of my alcoholism, I also _____ (insert substance, relationship problem or process addiction)."

The final ultimate concern is arguably the most anxiety provoking or all… death. It is an existential truth that we all must cease to exist, though most do not constantly ponder this inevitability. Many of the actions which we engage in, both adaptive and maladaptive can be related to this fact. Hence, we proceed through our life addressing our existential concerns trying to find meaning through responsible choices, ultimately cumulating in a legacy which *lives* on. Whether one's legacy is work related, socially focused, through one's offspring, or whatever other form it may take is dependent on our freedom of choice.

In line with a constructionistic view, it is often true that our perception of the truth that we associate with the awareness that life is finite, largely determines whether we engage in effective or non-effective behaviors as related to death. One can choose to engage in altruism, working with charities, for instance. On the other hand, compulsions or overcompensation may dominate one's actions. Again, it is the individual's responsibility to choose in what to engage in.

The alcoholic or addict's behavior in this regard could be said to be a non-effective response to the existential inevitability of death. Given these people's common disposition of defiance or rebellion, relinquishing one's control, in terms of a sense of safety could explain disordered substance use. F#*%!! death to sum it up. I cannot deny having heard such stories in the meeting rooms of the 12-step societies, or of having had these thoughts myself when I was drinking and using. Moreover, it seems that many of these individual's engage in extreme or what some may call reckless activities outside of substance abuse itself. These activities may include extreme sports, which can also be beneficial if approached with the proper frame of mind. Other times, however, extreme or risky actions take the form of other less beneficial activities such as gambling or speeding down the highway. Again, whether this recklessness is motivated by death's inevitability or needing a neurochemically induced jolt from the limbic system is difficult to say for sure, but there it is.

Fear of death and its certainty may however be a more likely factor in the alcoholic and addicts' actions and reactions. Fear, also known as anxiety, is a prominent topic of discussion in the meeting halls, as well as a key focus in the work which is done between sponsor and sponsee. Where or how this fear developed, or if it is motivated by existential concerns seems less important at the beginning of this work than as recovery progresses. It is certain that addressing one's fear is paramount. This is exemplified in that fear has a designated section to engage in during completion of the fourth step. At this point, the "Big Book" addresses fear thusly, "Fear somehow touched about every aspect of our lives. It was an evil and corroding thread; the fabric of our existence was shot through with it (Alcoholics Anonymous, 2001. Pp. 67-68.)." Fear as a motivator of problematic behavior, is highly evident in the lives of alcoholics, addicts, and those with mental health issues and must be addressed in recovery.

The 12-step programs, AA in particular, addresses fear with the hope of changing one's perspective of it, normalizing it and attempting to remove the power it has over the person. This is again, not unlike traditional psychotherapeutic modalities and is often an effective approach. The psychic change associated with the spiritual upheaval of one's belief and perspective is the goal. Bill supported this idea, writing in the January 1962 edition of the "Grapevine," that despite the destructiveness of fear, it can also be a steppingstone to greater things. ... the lesson of its consequences can lead to positive values."

The AA Responsibility Declaration threads the fabric of Existentialism's ultimate concerns in my opinion, further demonstrating the interconnectedness of today's therapeutic philosophies and the principles of the 12-step program. Unveiled at the international convention of 1965, it states, "I am responsible… When anyone, anywhere, reaches out for help, I want the hand of A.A. always to be there. And for that: I am responsible (Alcoholics Anonymous, 1967. Pp. 332)."

Humanistic Psychologies

Humanistic philosophies in psychology have a few concepts which are held in common. First, is the belief that humans are unique, creative beings and should be recognized as such. This is an emphasis on the idea that a person's experiences and the meaning he or she creates in association with those experiences, deeply influence that person's thoughts and actions. It is related to and leads to the next concept of Holism. Holism is a move away from the classical ideas of psychoanalysis and behavioralism. These reductionist perspectives are believed to reduce individuals into categories of symptoms or behaviors while disregarding the human experience. Another concept is contextualism. Contextualism asserts that human experience, or the context in which an event occurs or occurred influences the thinking and behavior people activate in the here and now. The focus on the here and now brings to bear the concepts previously spoken of. A here and now focus moves away from a rigid perspective about how a past event is driving certain thoughts and actions to one of more fluidity. As contexts are shifting consistently, so too are a person's perceptions of reality or what is true in the moment. Lastly, Humanistic philosophies champion the belief that people are innately motivated towards growth, self-improvement, and self-completion, also known as self-actualization.

Not unlike the ideas of Existentialism, Humanistic ideas are more of an additional ingredient used in psychotherapy versus a specific treatment modality. Alfred Adler is again influential in the incorporation of these ideas in therapy before they began gaining mainstream notoriety. His early influence can be seen in several other champions of the humanistic approach, such as Abraham Maslow, Fritz Perls, and Carl Rogers. Maslow joined with Heinz Ansbacher, an advocate for Adler's Individual Psychology approach, to identify six assertions of humanistic psychology; 1) people's creative power is a crucial force, in addition to heredity and environment, 2) a humanlike approach towards working with people is superior to a mechanical model, 3) purpose, rather than cause, is the decisive dynamic, 4) the holistic approach is more adequate than an elementaristic one, 5) it is necessary to take humans' subjectivity, their opinions and viewpoints, and their conscious and unconscious fully into account (holism), and 6) psychotherapy is essentially based on a good human relationship (Corsini, 2011).

A couple of the more well-known humanistic approaches are the Gestalt and Person-Centered methods. Aside from the humanistic perspectives entwined in the Person-Centered approach, other concepts are somewhat at odds with the 12-step approach to recovery. Most specifically, is the "hands off," non-directive relationship style which the Person-Centered therapist takes. This approach is somewhat inconsistent with how most sponsors work with their sponsees. Again, this is not to suggest that a sponsor is in anyway a trained therapist or is providing the same service, aside from the relationship. This is also not to say that for some individuals a non-directive approach is not necessary or effective. Generally speaking, in my experience it seems a more active and direct relationship is more effective in working with addicts and alcoholics. The alcoholic, addict, or whatever issue a person is seeking help with in a 12-step program is generally out of answers, or has it a bottom, and is seeking and in need of direction. As such, the Person-Centered approach may be too passive.

Now, I will discuss the basic principles of Gestalt theory and how they relate to 12-step principles and can be usefully incorporated into the program. First is organismic self-regulation. To sum, organismic self-regulation requires that one be in touch with themselves. That is an understanding of one's needs, both emotional and physical, as well as what one believes, sees, and feels. It also requires that a person accepts or owns these characteristics of the self. Organismic self-regulation also requires and understanding of what is happening in one's daily life, as well as how a person is affecting others. Gestalt therapy asserts that growth begins with this awareness, as well as a willingness to be honest with oneself about what is occurring in their life.

This awareness of a connection with the self is generally absent, if not limited in individuals seeking aid with troubling circumstances in their lives. When limited, the connections to personal convictions are often skewed by mistaken ideas that lead to incongruence of self or essentially disconnection with the self. As such, acceptance through surrender, a key concept in 12-step recovery, begins the process of change, also known as growth. Surrender and willingness are surmised in the idea that we (12-step members) have commenced to stop fighting everything and everyone (Alcoholics Anonymous, 2001). A daily inventory of self (Step 10) is an integral part of surrender, willingness, and long-term sobriety/recovery and is in line with the Gestalt concept of staying connected to the self and one's personal convictions.

Acceptance through surrender is then the key, or at least *a* key to recovery. *The* Dr. Paul (not me), an AA icon, surmised that acceptance is the key to a person's serenity. Dr. Paul's famous (as far as anonymous fame is concerned) assertion is that the level of acceptance a person uses versus the level of discord they may be experiencing directly effects the level of serenity, or peace of mind that same person will experience in the here and now. Honesty, Open-mindedness, Willingness (H.O.W.), an AA acronym, is *how* it (the program of recovery) is done and is also crucial in gaining acceptance. Honesty, open-mindedness, and willingness are required to begin one's journey towards wholeness in the 12-step societies. With that said, I would argue that honesty, open-mindedness, and willingness are required to make progress in traditional psychotherapy as well.

The concept of the Paradoxical Theory of Change is a central part of Gestalt therapy. In effect, the paradox is that the harder one wishes or tries to change, the more they stay the same. Gestalt theory posits that healing occurs through the process making oneself whole again. This is made more difficult by the fact that the individual is prone to feeling incongruent because they are not whole. Typically, this fragmented sense of self is exacerbated by trying to force change upon a person.

Hence, as passive, non-directive approach is used to allow the person's innate desire for self-completion promote self-direction. Again, where alcoholics and addicts are concerned, this may not be the most effective approach. Nonetheless, it is a notable concept.

As previously discussed, this feeling of fragmentation or of feeling incomplete is often discussed in the meeting rooms in which I have been present. The idea is expressed in statements of "feeling less than...," or in "having a hole in the soul," or as simply as feeling empty inside. The Paradoxical Theory of Change is a bit paradoxical in how it is enacted by sponsors. As the concept is essentially non-directive, in terms of trying to force change, the sponsor takes a subtle...*ish* directive approach. The sponsor does this by encouraging/directing the newcomer to go to meetings and complete the step work. This eventually brings about the changes required to make the person whole again as a result of other program dynamics. Some of these dynamics are humanistic in nature, such as unconditional positive regard which is expressed in meetings as related to the person's primary issue. The hole in the soul is filled. The human spirit returns. The person feels more like a complete human; he or she is whole again. If only it were that simple. Or is it? It may be that simple, however it is a process and with any process some may benefit more rapidly than others.

The here and now focus is expressed in the motto, "a day at a time." Not only does this focus the individual on being mindful and present in the moment, but also alleviates the stress of committing to abstinence for the rest of a person's life, which can be helpful. Existing in the here and now facilitates a person's ability to accept or change circumstances in their lives that they find less than desirable, while also alleviating the anxiety of being future focused. Conscious awareness is a goal of Gestalt therapy and 12-step programs alike, helping people stay in the moment. There is wide consensus that people who live (focus) in the past tend to be depressed, while people who live (focus) in the future tend to be anxious.

Another area in which Gestalt therapy and 12-step principles align is in the idea of experimentation, as related to new behaviors. The benefit of increased understanding of self and others is possible through engagement in new activities. People may become more aware of their emotional states as a result. People often engage in the same pattern of unsatisfying, useless behavior and complain about it, without really being aware. It has become comfortable to them. The concept of doing the same thing over and over, while expecting different result becomes operable here. Though not exclusively a 12-step principle, the idea is a visible point of discussion in and out of meetings.

The Gestalt therapist suggests different actions, while the sponsor *strongly* suggests actions. That is to say, when a person is working with a sponsor, the sponsor's suggestions are more directive. This is again related to the idea of surrender and acceptance that the newcomer has resigned some of his or her will to the care of the sponsor during the growth process which seeks to aid the individual in better understanding themselves. I was told by my sponsor that I would be fine if I just did the opposite of what I thought I should do in terms of new behavior and old behavior for that matter. If I did not want to take a commitment, I should take a commitment and the like. This is a way of getting the newcomer to engage in new activities and have new experiences which are likely to increase congruence and support the recovery process.

Behavioralism

Alcoholism and addiction are considered by many professionals to be a behavior or behavioral pattern and can argue that those with mental health issues without substance abuse are in a pattern of maladaptive behaviors, as well. It is true that there a many behavioral cycles with which alcoholics and addicts engage. A common one is related to distressed feelings. The alcoholic/addict engages in drink or drug use and experiences a feeling of relief. Given the nature of addiction they lose control and create more strife through their actions, both substance related and relationally. Subsequently they wake or re-emerge with more distress associated with the loss of control and problems they created during the last binge and start the whole cycle all over again due to the increased distress. The AA concept of being "unable to live life on life's terms," or behave in a manner conducive to creating a satisfying life seems applicable here. However, the basic principles of Behavioralism are rewards and punishments. This is where the waters become clouded, as related to alcoholism and addiction, because the reward eventually becomes punishing.

As it is apparent that behavior plays a large role in the lives of alcoholics and addicts, the term does open the door for the debate as to the voracity of the claim that said syndromes are purely behavioral issues based on reward versus punishment. At the time in which AA was forming, alcoholism was considered by most outside the medical fraternity as a moral issue related to self-control or applying the will. Others consider cognition, distorted thinking and misguided perceptions to be responsible.

When looking at the word alcohol*ism*, it seems that it is more likely a combination of these things. Words which contain the suffix *-ism*, according to dictionary.com are defined as, a distinctive doctrine, theory, system, or practice. An explanation of the origin indicates that the Greeks used it to form action-oriented nouns which suggests a behavior. It continues, stating it is a production suffix denoting a practice, state or condition, principles, doctrine, and a devotion or adherence to…, suggesting a combination of thought and action.

The behavioral school of thought in psychology is represented by the concepts of learning through operant and classical conditioning, known as modern learning theory. Early behavioral approaches to therapy could be defined as the use of modern learning theory to treat mental health issues in the clinical setting (Corsini, 2011). Modern learning theory is largely based on the interactions between a person's actions and the results or consequences of those actions. The operating premise being… if an action results in a favorable consequence, then the action will be repeated and vice versa. The theory makes sense. Does it not? It seems reasonable that I am more inclined to do things I like doing or get a reward for. There is an underlying dilemma, however. What about something like exercise or studying? Many people would say that they enjoy engaging in said activity. For others, they may not enjoy the activity per se, however it is the results or rewards they enjoy, which prolongs or induces repetition of the behavior. For those in 12-step programs this underlying dilemma is at the heart of whatever behavior they are seeking help for. With alcohol and drugs, the maladaptive cycle was illustrated previously. The reward is the relief of inherent distress, described by Dr. Silkworth as feeling restless, irritable, and discontent (Alcoholics Anonymous, 2001). This behavior works for a while by providing the desired relief equaling a positive consequence. As per modern learning theory this behavior is continued. However, something happens as time passes. Some of the possibilities have been previously discussed, and the distress returns. As the distress returns, usage increases, eventually leading to less desired consequences in the person's work and home lives creating again more distress. As previously stated, the waters of reward and punishment become clouded.

It is a common understanding in 12-step societies that alcohol and drugs were the solution to the person's problems, however this solution eventually became an additional problem. A therapist I worked with described this reward cycle as, "Fun. Then fun with problems. Then eventually just problems." I believe this to be true with more process related 12-step oriented societies, as well. This is the point of contention in treating alcoholism and addiction from a purely behavioral perspective. This approach may be more successful in working with people with mental health issues minus the substance abuse because the reward and the truth become obscured from the alcoholic and addict. This is not to say that those without substance dependence are not prone to an obscured perspective and the difficulty of being objective when viewing their own behavior. However, the relief of distress, or fallacy of relief, as addiction progresses, shrouds the multiplying problems the addiction has and is creating.

There has emerged from the behavioral school of thought several more intricate philosophies which incorporate cognitive dynamics into the behavioral modification process. This, in my opinion, is a more effective approach, as it is the thinking of people in recovery which tends to complicate the simplest of concepts. People appear for counseling/ therapy, or at a treatment center seeking help and believing they are motivated to do so. Yet when encouraged to change problematic behavior, they do not, often wondering why nothing has changed.

Dialectical Behavioral Therapy (DBT) and Acceptance and Commitment Therapy (ACT) are the most notable approaches to emerge from the modern learning theory model. DBT was created by Marsha Linehan specifically to treat individuals with borderline personality disorder but has been found effective in treating other disorders and with "difficult" clients. Anyone who has worked or lived with an alcoholic or addict can attest that these individuals can be difficult (even when sober). Acceptance of change and mindfulness are cornerstones of the DBT process. Interestingly, Corsini cites the Serenity Prayer in a section which discusses acceptance. The Serenity Prayer is a cornerstone of recovery in the 12-step societies. So, it would seem, DBT is in line with the principles of 12-step recovery to some extent. The basic tenants of DBT; Mindfulness, Interpersonal Effectiveness,

Distress Tolerance, and Emotional Regulation are indeed helpful in recovery; no matter which environment or for what mental disorder one may be seeking help with. However, having had training by the county's local DBT clinic, I do see some drawbacks.

The crux of the difficulty with alcoholics and addicts is the previously discussed mindset of seeking an easier, softer way to whatever ends they may be seeking. *True* DBT, as a therapeutic approach is highly structured and entails much homework and therapeutic written interventions. All this homework and structure may be discouraging to the alcoholic/addict, who are often seeking *an easier, softer way*. This may likely be true in non-substance abusing clinical populations as well.

I say *true* DBT work, as nearly every clinic I have practiced in has a DBT group… once a week, for 90 minutes. Then advertise on their websites that they are DBT clinics or provide DBT treatment (the ethics of this practice is a discussion for another time). That is not DBT treatment. That is teaching the principles of DBT. I endorse the principles of DBT, as learning and employing them is likely to help improve people's lives. However, DBT is highly structured and builds concepts on top of concepts to facilitate the learning and practice of more productive behavior. If one can galvanize a commitment by the individual to participate and maintain their motivation, *true* DBT has been shown to produce effective results.

A final potential handicap which may be present in DBT when considering alcoholics and addicts is the idea of "being cool." Many alcoholics and addicts expend a great deal of energy in maintaining an identity of "being cool." That may be related to the day's trends, hobbies, or whatever may facilitate the feeling and likely stems from the previously discussed absence of self-esteem. It could be identity related, in terms of why the individual started using substances in the first place; to be "cool," or to do what the "cool" people are doing. On a deeper level, it may be motivated more by a need to be accepted by others. That idea combined with a highly external focus and searching for an easier softer way may prove problematic when trying to incorporate the instructional acronyms associated with DBT. I recall the grumbling and jests during groups in which I was trying to teach the concept of D.E.A.R.M.A.N.

Moving on, let us look at Acceptance and Commitment Therapy (ACT). ACT employs several useful overlaps with the 12-step recovery programs. Obviously, acceptance is a key concept which can facilitate recovery. Acceptance of not only the nature of alcoholism/addiction and the characteristics of said individual, but of the conditions of life; "living life on life's terms" to be exact.

The ACT concept of Experiential Avoidance posits a behavioral pattern of avoiding uncomfortable experiences. The idea of being uncomfortable in one's skin is highly endorsed in the meetings I have attended and have experienced personally. Isolation which could be considered the ultimate avoidance is also a topic of discussion which receives an abundance of agreeing nods and "um-hmms" in meeting discussions. Avoidance of one's thoughts and/or feelings is also spoken of frequently. I have heard many 12-step members discuss the need to "shut off their head."

The next premise of ACT, Cognitive Diffusion is another overlapping concept. Cognitive Diffusion encourages the separating of thoughts from the self in order to enact more appropriate responses. A common slogan which was extremely helpful in my own recovery is, "I am not responsible for my first thought, but I am responsible for my next thought and my action." This slogan, in my opinion, embodies the idea of Cognitive Diffusion. Learning to employ this concept can lead to more beneficial decision making. It surely has done this in my life.

Finally, is Commitment. In the framework of ACT, commitment refers to making mindful decisions as related to the forming of a satisfying life. Commitment in the 12-step societies seem more behavioral in nature, though the basis and primary goal is that of seeking satisfaction in one's life. 12-step commitments, as discussed, entail involvement at both the behavioral and relational levels of the society, while ACT discusses mindful *decisions*. At the risk of appearing to be splitting the proverbial hairs, I will assert that making mindful decisions is not enough. Alcoholics and addicts (and those with other mental health issues) make decisions to change their behavior, all the time. But the question is more appropriately directed to the extent in which they engage the behaviors necessary to support that decision. Decisions do not necessarily mean acting, although *deciding* is the emphasis of the third step. My sponsor posed this brain twister to me at that point. He said, "There are five birds sitting on a branch above a bird bath. Three of them *decided* to go down and take a bath. How many birds are left on the branch?" The immediate answer for me was… two. However, he indicated that five remained on the branch, as they had only *decided* to fly down to the bath. The birds did not yet take any action related to that decision. Hence, they did not engage in any productive behavior. Nonetheless, the productive behavior begins after making the Third Step decision. The Fourth Step is when the individual takes the action or engages in the behavior of deconstruction of self, which eventually leads to the building of self-*acceptance*. From this point begins to emerge a new and productive perspective of self, life and how one can successfully navigate and relate to self and life.

Cognitive Behavioral Theory/Therapy

Cognitive Behavioral Therapy (CBT), or sometimes referred to as simply Cognitive Therapy is the darling of insurance companies, owners of clinics, and program directors who are clamoring for empirically supported interventions to satisfy the voracious appetites of the prior. I *may* argue that all the theories/philosophies in psychology are cognitive, but I digress. Many aspects of CBT, as we will discuss, are highly effective and provide results. Nonetheless, Corsini's book on current psychotherapies has an evidence of efficacy section for each philosophical perspective, suggesting that it is less about what type of therapy one engages, than it is about other factors, such as the client/therapist alliance/relationship.

CBT seems to me to be a hijacking of one of Adler's primary concepts, the mistaken belief, in terms of effective thinking and behaving as he presented in his Individual Psychology. What's the difference between a thought distortion and a mistaken belief, besides the terminology? Again, I digress.

Let us continue exploring CBT, as there are subtleties between them. These subtleties are mainly related to the "depth" in which one dissects the reasons a person has arrived at these mistaken beliefs; oops… I mean thought distortions. CBT/Cognitive Theory is less concerned with "the why" (thoughts are formed) and more concerned with "the how" thoughts are affecting a person's life in terms of emotions and behavior. This is significant, as related to the program of recovery described in the AA "Big Book."

New members are often engaged in the unproductive seeking of the rationale behind the problematic drinking (drugging, or process) behavior. Sponsors often point out that this is the "ism," or disease attempting to distract them from what matters. What matters is engaging in new behavior. As such, it seems that AA is less concerned with why a person arrived at their rooms, than they are with engaging new behavior and new thinking; or vice versa.

The cognitive theories rely heavily on the concept of information processing. The processing of information is linked to an individual's survival, in the sense of gathering and assessing said information. Further processing leads the individual in formulating a plan of action which he or she believes is the course likely to produce the most effective outcome. Thusly, engaging in the behavior which the person has discerned as most likely to achieve the desired outcome. This system would be wonderful and produce consistently desirable results if not for one's inevitable application of experience. That said experience is the influence of one's cumulative hurts, pleasures, knowledge, beliefs, and any other potential influences on a person's cognitive make up. These experiences make the process less simple and less wonderful.

Cognitive oriented therapists believe that through our experience a person forms cognitive biases based on how they interpret (misinterpret) or process the information. For example, people prone to depression, view life with a negative or pessimistic bias. Biases manifest and perpetuate in other mental health disorders through these associated biases as well. For instance, pessimism can also influence anxiety feelings, but not manifest into depression based on one's belief, as related to self-efficacy. A person with anxiety may simply worry about or catastrophize life and life's potential situations. While the depressed person does not believe that they, the individual can affect or improve the situation, thus becoming filled with hopelessness. This idea is consistent with the previously mentioned constructionist view, which posits that a person *constructs* their reality through their thinking and subsequent *story* they associate with it. In some people the reality or story that is constructed is useful and effective, with others the reality can become distorted. This is especially true when the stories are created in a person's developmental stages of life. Hence, the augmented effects on behavior which tend to be observed in those who have had traumatic experiences as young children (but this concept is less important in CBT).

Although less concerned with why the thoughts developed, CBT does posit that said experiences form our personal mind set, perspectives and perceptions, which can again become distorted in the mind's attempt to relieve the self from discomfort. For instance, it is often easier (more comfortable) for some to believe a fabricated excuse for a shortcoming or failure, than it is to face the truth which generally resides in the consciousness of self. "The truth hurts" is a common quote for good reason. Eventually, what used to reside in the consciousness is obscured by biases and distortions creating more discomfort in a disconnection with oneself. This is what humanistic philosophies call incongruence. Another truthful platitude is "denial is not just a river in Egypt." Denial though commonly considered a defense mechanism is also or can be considered a cognitive distortion (CBT's word for defense mechanism). Justification, intellectualization, and rationalization are some common thought or cognitive distortions which many people use to make themselves feel less distressed when they fall short of a desired mark or are hurt in some way.

This is significant because for some people the truth is often so uncomfortable that it becomes exceedingly difficult to interact and relate to others without using the veil of cognitive distortions. This is not only true in alcoholics and addicts, but this un-comfortability may be experienced more acutely by this population. A person's perception can become so skewed that the resulting behavior is also skewed, moving from functional to dysfunctional. Hence, when dysfunctional information processing is active, it is reasonable to assume that dysfunctional behavior will follow as a result. This is the metaphorical heart of CBT and Cognitive Psychotherapies. Again, CBT and Cognitive Psychotherapies focus less on why the dysfunction is present, rather than with changing dysfunctional processing to more functional processing. As a result, more functional behavior logically follows more functional processing.

At a somewhat deeper level, as far as CBT is concerned, is the concept of a person's core beliefs. These beliefs are often assumptions formed from experienced biases about the self, others and the world.

In those who are experiencing difficulties relating to themselves, the world and others it is fair to surmise that their core beliefs contain many cognitive distortions. When core beliefs are invalidated or disputed either by directly experiencing something contradictory to their beliefs or through the introduction of a contrary idea, more distress is triggered. At this point, the person is required to deal with this contradiction in their belief system. One way to do this is by creating more cognitive distortions. The discomfort of the phenomena of experiencing something contrary to one's core beliefs is known as cognitive dissonance. Roughly defined, cognitive dissonance is the space (cognitively speaking, of course) between a person's core belief and their experienced reality. Consequently, this space or gap is anxiety provoking, as the individual is tasked with either changing their related belief or creating more distortions to fit it in to their reality.

Cognitive distortions can be effective in relieving psychic distress and though I am reluctant to say *all* people use them... all people use them. However, the difference between mentally healthy versus mentally unhealthy is often a matter of degree. We all use cognitive distortions from time to time, as stated, but their use can become problematic when an individual allows themselves to be dominated by this type of thinking. Cognitive distortions are effective in small doses and are even beneficial in coping with setbacks and in constructing the mindset to carry on when life gives us proverbial lemons. Denial is, in fact the first stage in the grieving process. This not by accident, but because cognitive distortions work in the alleviation of distress.

However, in large doses cognitive distortions lose their effectiveness. In the case of the grieving process, one must eventually move on from denial to effectively grieve and return to effective functioning. Alcohol and drugs serve as a shortcut of sorts in the relieving of cognitive distress, however when the effects subside, the alcoholic/addict often employs many cognitive distortions to alleviate uncomfortable feelings. These feelings can be associated with life's responsibilities or about their addictive behaviors.

Metaphorically, one can liken problematic use of cognitive distortions to the building of a card house. Each card is a cognitive distortion alleviating some distress or another. At times, these stress alleviating cards are multiplied; as they are distortions meant to alleviate the stress which previously activated distortions did not fully relieve, thus compounding the ineffectiveness. The card house grows taller and more unstable as more distortions are needed to handle disappointments and dissonance. Until eventually, the card house crumbles.

A person's learned experiences coupled with their desires and needs form reactionary patterns known as schemas. When a current experience triggers the reaction or activation of an established schema, the person engages in the prescribed behavior. These reactions tend to become automatic. Automatic thoughts are an area which Cognitive therapists focus on with their clients, as automatic thoughts lead to automatic behaviors. These automatic behaviors are often the reason that people are living troubled or unsatisfying lives. The results or consequences of schema driven actions tend to confirm the core beliefs of the individual, subsequently providing some relief despite unfavorable outcomes.

This is where more depth is required in my opinion. One may ask how unfavorable outcomes can provide relief. As related to one's core beliefs, it is entirely possible. For instance, if a person believes they are worthless (as a core belief) an outcome considered favorable would lead to feelings of worth in the said person, if common sense were applied. However, this is a conflict deep within a person whose core belief is that they are worthless. Most likely this belief resides in the unconscious or preconscious mind leaving the person unaware of its existence. This creates internal distress in the individual as it confronts their identity as a worthless person. It is somewhat of a paradox. That person takes automatic actions fueled by automatic thoughts that create distress in the consciousness but soothes the unconscious belief that they are worthless. This is the reason people in treatment often do not take the prescribed actions of a therapist, or sponsor for that matter. The familiar distress is more comfortable than the unknown outcome of taking a new and different action.

This is where the CBT practitioner says to the client, "It does not matter *why* you feel worthless. If you take this prescribed action (contrary to the schema pattern), it may feel distressing at first. However, with practice, the distress will transform into peace of mind." Although this is a deliberately vague example, this is how the concept of action in terms of contrary behavior comes into play, as related to recovery from addiction (and other mental health issues) within my stated opinion.

A saying I learned in the rooms of AA relates and surmises this idea. "You can't think your way into good acting, but you can act your way into good thinking."

That is how a person changes unproductive and ineffective thinking, either in or out of AA (or other 12-Step programs). Action. As previously discussed, action is what changes a person's belief system. That is, taking an action, having a new experience, which then changes a person's story or core beliefs. This story is how the person perceives the world and their life in relation to it. The action that I am speaking of is contrary action. Contrary meaning that the person does not want to do it. This is the understanding as related to Cognitive Theory/CBT and the paradox of schemas, as well as 12-Step recovery. This is also pivotal in the sponsor/sponsee relationship. The sponsor has had the experience of doing things they did not want to do when they were a newcomer, as prescribed by their sponsor. The sponsor understands, more through experience than the technicalities explained above, how the process works and how the process has aided him/her in changing core beliefs and unproductive behavior.

Addiction and alcoholism can be viewed from this perspective, even when ruling out the potential physiological component to addiction. As previously noted, many in the field of psychology see addiction as a behavior; cost/benefit analysis, if you will. More precisely the cost/benefit is related to punishment and reinforcement from the behavioral view. Given the aforementioned dynamic related to core beliefs and how they impact what a person may view as punishment or reward, behavioral outcomes become clouded. What is more, the pleasurable relief (at the physiological and psychological level) provided by alcohol and drugs is so elusive it may be a reward regardless of the collateral damage it is causing in a person's life.

The cycle of uncomfortable thoughts leading to uncomfortable feelings leads to drinking/using behavior in which the individual finds relief is commonly known as the addiction cycle. As the cycle continues, tolerance and progression processes occur even though the DSM-V no longer acknowledges this. Next as the cycle continues, undesirable circumstances begin to manifest in the alcoholics' life creating more uncomfortable thoughts and feelings which require higher doses to alleviate. So forth this continues until a "bottom," which is as different as the individual is reached. It starts as fun; becomes fun with problems; eventually becoming only problems. This is the cycle of addiction or alcoholism in a nutshell. Though it is safe to say, the details and duration of this journey are as varied as the human species, it is essentially the root of the process, in my opinion. At the risk of seeming cynical, the cycle somewhat resembles the medical model for treating mental health disorders. Of course, this is without an action orientation related to new learning coupled with decreasing titration of medication.

It is a well-known parameter in the rooms of AA and other 12-Step programs that the program is action oriented. Again, "I cannot think my way into good acting, but I can act my way into good thinking." A well-known Adlerian intervention is called as "Act as if." Feelings are not facts; a well-known motto in CBT affirms the efficacy behind acting as if. If a person acts despite (or *in* spite of) how they feel about it, it is likely the false feelings and thoughts will change. This is the basic tenant behind the benefit of taking a sponsor's direction and often a topic of contention in the professional treatment arena. Obviously, most sponsors are not trained professionals. There are times when some sponsors overstep boundaries, but the general AA premise behind sponsorship, as related to a sponsor's duties, is focused on helping the individual move through and complete the steps while remaining abstinent. Moreover, the "Big Book" specifically encourages those with problems outside this realm, for example psychological, medical, religious or legal, to seek out the appropriate professional for assistance.

Al-Anon, Adult Children of Alcoholics, and Emotions Anonymous

It has been said that living by the principles of the 12-Step program outlined by Alcoholics Anonymous is beneficial for anyone. Anyone being the so-called "normies" who do not have a problem with alcohol, substances or other process-oriented addictions. One could hypothesize the 12-Step philosophy is an effective way to live. In my opinion and experience, this seems to be accurate. First is my experience of using the 12-Steps to facilitate my own recovery and re-engagement with a satisfying life. Secondly, my experience in working as a psychotherapist and with people who were un-addicted.

The principles, such as humility and letting go are guidelines in both the rooms of 12-Step societies and the rooms of clinical psychology. More importantly, 12-Step recovery is a transformation of beliefs, actions and attitudes that lead to a more peaceful life when successfully applied. 12-Step recovery is a transformation of a person's identity, which is one of the most difficult processes in psychotherapy. It is deeper than the simple application of better coping skills, although applying new coping skills is part of the process. It is less of a recovery program, than it is a style of living.

The book Alcoholics Anonymous describes untreated alcoholism displayed by the alcoholic as, '…having trouble with our relationships, we couldn't control our emotional natures, we were a prey to misery and depression, we couldn't make a living, we had a feeling of uselessness, we were full of fear, we were unhappy, we couldn't seem to be of real help to other people… (Alcoholics Anonymous, 2001. Pp. 52)." These are known within the AA society as the "bedevilments (as stated further in the paragraph)" and are common symptoms people experience. Dr. Silkworth surmised the bedevilments as a disposition of being restless, irritable and discontent. Does this not describe many, if not all people who are seeking mental health treatment with or without substance abuse issues? Perhaps this is a description of the human condition! The differential crux of the problem being how a person deals with this condition. The point being… adopting and acting in harmony with the prescribed principles alleviates these bedevilments or uncomfortable states of mind and being. This supports the notion that the principles of the 12-Step program can be useful tools for living with peace of mind and aligned with the principles employed by psychotherapy.

Members of the various 12-Step societies, especially the substance-oriented programs often attend other groups in conjunction with the group that they identify as their "main" problem. For instance, an Alcoholic who has a gambling problem may attend AA and GA. Here too, the guidance and experience of a sponsor proves useful. If one applies the psychodynamic concepts of projection or identification, one could argue that a new person chooses a sponsor for these reasons. With that in mind, the sponsor often sees and understands a new person's characteristics and makes suggestions to aid in helping with these other "character defects." Interaction with other members, especially "old-timers" is another avenue in which members seek out other 12-Step programs for help with troubling issues.

An event like this took place in my own recovery. I was interacting with an old-timer who had something like 35 years of sobriety at the time and attended a men's meeting I frequented. This man was an acquaintance of Dr. Claudia Black, a pioneer psychologist who focused on the dynamics of Adult Children of Alcoholics (ACA). Dr. Black, in her pioneering years worked with this man. As a result, he noticed some of the "quirks" in my character and suggested that once I had more time in sobriety, it might be a helpful experience for me if I attended their meetings. Though he was not a mental health professional himself, he was aware of the strong emotional nature of this group. That is why he suggested that I wait until I was more mature in my own sobriety before embarking on what may have been too much (from an emotional standpoint) for me at that early stage in my sobriety. He cared enough about me to not want to jeopardize my sobriety, but at the same time gave me something to think about. Eventually, I did end up attending and becoming a member of ACA. This experience was a wonderful learning and healing venture which has also helped me in becoming a more competent and comprehensive therapist, as well as an overall person, friend and son.

Nowadays, as a result of the success of Alcoholics Anonymous, a person can find a 12-Step group for just about any issues that one is experiencing. Though there are many groups listed when conducting a search, finding an actual meeting for some of the more obscure societies may be difficult, if not impossible in more rural areas. However, one benefit of the current pandemic is that these meetings are now available through web communications and people living in rural areas need only attain a meeting guide from more urban areas to receive the benefits of attending. I often suggest this to patients who are having difficulty finding some of the more obscure 12-step societies. Hopefully when the pandemic subsides, these more obscure variants in 12-step recovery will continue to convene in online forums for those less fortunately situated.

A discussion of all the categories which are available is somewhat beyond useful purpose, but a discussion of the more readily available groups is not. The most notable are, of course the substance related societies; Alcoholics Anonymous (AA), Narcotics Anonymous (NA), Cocaine Anonymous (CA) and Marijuana Anonymous (MA) to name a few. As far as the relationship and process societies are concerned, we will take a look at Al-Anon, Adult Children of Alcoholics (ACA), and Emotions Anonymous (EA). Some of the better-known groups which will not be discussed but indicate the conditions they focus on in the name include, Codependents Anonymous (CODA), Overeaters Anonymous (OA), Gamblers Anonymous (GA). Computer Gaming Addicts Anonymous (CGAA), and Sex and Love Addicts Anonymous (SLAA) to name a scant few.

Al-Anon is a group/society whose purpose is to assist the families and friends of people who are recovering or practicing alcoholics and addicts. A sub-group of Al-Anon is called Alateen. Alateen essentially uses the principle of Al-Anon but is specific to the teenaged (or near teenaged) children from such families. Adults are generally not a part of the Alateen group make up.

Dr. Bob's wife Anne, was active in working with the families of alcoholics since before the roots of AA began to grow as a result of that meeting between her husband and Bill W. However, Anne S. had died in 1949. The Al-Anon family groups were co-founded by Bill W's wife, Lois and Anne B., the wife of another member at the time. It is said that Lois, despite understanding the importance of Bill's work in AA and her own desire for his sobriety, had become frustrated with going to meetings with him. One Sunday afternoon these feelings, which she had been repressing for some time had exploded from her for no apparent reason leading her to examine her own attitudes. As such, she realized that the families of the individuals who were attending AA could benefit from the very spiritual principles which were helping their alcoholic loved ones recover.

In 1951, following a large AA convention, Lois decided to form an organization for the families of recovering alcoholics. Hence, Lois and Anne B, researched and reviewed the names of people who had reached out to AA with questions about alcoholism. These people were not the alcoholics themselves, but the family members of alcoholics. Lois and Anne contacted them for discussions of their problems. This is the point in time which is associated with the formation of Al-Anon Family Groups. (Wilson, 1995).

Expanding on the brief description of the purpose of Al-Anon

Family Groups provided earlier, it is appropriate to review how the group describes itself. "Al-Anon is an independent fellowship with the stated purpose of helping relatives and friends of alcoholics (www.al-anon.org.)." A common misconception is that Al-Anon helps people help the alcoholic/addict to stop drinking or using, however this is not the case. Lois believed that as a result of the alcoholic's behavior, people close to them were distressed by these experiences and needed emotional support themselves (Wilson, 1995).

Codependency, a common characteristic of those with addicted loved ones, was first conceptualized via Al-Anon. The concept of codependency and the characteristics of the codependent individual, also referred to as enabling has been an area of much research in the field of psychology. This research has found that codependent characteristics exist in many environments outside the homes of addicted individuals. For instance, codependent behavior is also common in the homes of those with other mental health disorders besides alcoholism and drug dependence and in dysfunctional families. It often appears in the alcoholic/addict themselves and when noticed by sponsors or others in the 12-Step societies, the codependents are encouraged to attend Al-Anon to support growth in this area. Some of the more enlightened treatment centers encourage or even require that clinicians and support workers attend Al-Anon groups to help in maintaining a more objective position when working with their clients.

Learning the principles of powerlessness and acceptance are key concepts in 12-Step recovery, although in Al-Anon the member is powerless over the behaviors of others, specifically their alcoholic family member. Al-Anon uses the 12-Steps in aiding its members achieve more satisfying and effective lives by increasing their serenity and peace of mind. Subsequently, studies conducted by Wright (1978) and Corsenblum (1975) indicate that when the alcoholic is active in AA and the partner/family is active in Al-Anon; 1) long term sobriety/abstinence is more likely, 2) happiness within the relationship is likely to improve, and 3) parenting is more likely to improve by both parties.

Adult Children of Alcoholics (ACA or sometimes ACOA) recently expanded to Adult Children of Alcoholics and Dysfunctional Families is another helpful 12-Step society. This group is an off shoot of Al-Anon, but they are separate entities. In my understanding, the addition of dysfunctional families is the result of new research findings which began with Dr. Claudia Black and was expounded upon by other researchers. These new findings indicate that children of families with a parent or parents suffering from severe mental health disorders manifest many of the same characteristics as those raised in alcoholic families.

These characteristics were summed up and illustrated in what the founder, Tony A. called "The Laundry List." These characteristics center around trust issues, unhealthy family dynamics and a damaged inner child. As a result of the parents' presenting issues, these children were called upon to be the caretakers of said parent(s), hence they essentially lost their childhoods. This is known as a parentified child, meaning that the responsibility of the parent was placed on the child. Often these responsibilities include, calling in sick for the parent, preparing meals, cleaning up after and putting the parent to bed to name a few. These experiences coupled with the nature of the malady often produce shame and could have been traumatic in nature. What is more, the family characteristic is one based on secrecy and isolation. As a result, the (adult) child learns to bury their true feelings while in school or other social gatherings. These suppressed feelings often manifest later in life, influencing their relationship choices and dynamics of the individual. Generally, an adult child seeks out someone to care for at their own expense in an unhealthy and unsatisfying manner. This is commonly associated with codependency. Some may become alcoholics, other substance abusers and/or addicted to various processes (often excitement or recklessness-oriented processes).

Though ACA is a 12-Step group/society, there is a more therapeutic nature displayed in group meetings. Much of the work focuses on reparenting one's wounded inner child in order to build self-efficacy and gain insight leading to more effective and satisfying life choices, especially in terms of relationships. There is a focus on learning new coping skills and taking responsibility for one's life versus maintaining a stance of victimhood, despite being victimized as children. Members encourage each other to learn and employ self-care, while standing up for their right to have satisfying relationships and a productive life (www.adultchildren.org).

As is the nature of 12-Step recovery programs, action is the key to change. Transformative action in ACA meetings takes the form of psychoeducation, skills building, emotional support and encouragement.

ACA has their version of AA's "Big Book," known as "The Big Red Book." ACA does not rely as heavily on the sponsorship dynamic as in other 12-Step groups, rather it is more of an atmosphere of mutual helping. Members share their experiences coupled with the solutions they discovered through learning and in the productive actions they have engaged in (www.adultchildren.org). Smith (1992) found that ACA involvement is a useful adjunct to traditional therapy, as it provides support in between therapy sessions.

Emotions Anonymous (EA) is a 12-Step program which focuses less upon substances and difficulties which arise from a person's relationships with individuals who abuse them, as it does on an individual's struggles with the emotional dysregulation caused by mental health issues. I was unaware of EA until my work took me to my most recent treatment clinic. I was working with mental health track patients for the most part, as I wanted more experience outside the dual diagnosis (addiction) population. EA was the foundation of this program track, as AA/NA was for the dual diagnosis population. What I discovered upon reading the EA "Big Book" made sense considering the characteristics displayed by the mental health track individuals. They were essentially powerless over their emotions which subsequently lead to poor decision making and dissatisfaction with their lives. The results of these poor decisions had led to work, family and relationships problems. That sounds a lot like the results of alcohol and substance addiction described as the bedevilments.

EA sprung from another 12-Step program, Neurotics Anonymous.

I am not sure of the details, but as students, we were encouraged to move away from using the term neurotic. It is possible that this was the reason for the shift, but again I am only speculating. What is import is that EA, as described appears to be a useful adjunct to traditional psychotherapy. This point is made clear in the EA preamble. EA is not a replacement for treatment, especially for those who have more severe forms of mental health disorders. Nonetheless, EA provides support, learning and encouragement between sessions. What is more, the process of letting go and having a spiritual awakening is likely to lead to better coping and an improved state of mind, in my opinion.

EA uses the 12-Step process in a similar manner as AA. The focus of one's powerlessness is on their emotions rather that alcohol, drugs, processes or relationships. In taking the steps, a person can deconstruct and identify exactly how the manifestation of emotion is unmanageable, in terms of a reaction to stimuli. However, a person can learn to respond more productively to uncontrollable emotional reactions. This is accomplished by engaging in a more productive behavioral response, versus the usual pattern of reacting to one's first thought or feeling. The EA insight building process also acknowledges the idea of a "three-fold disease/disorder." That is the recognition that emotional processes are linked dynamically through physical, mental and spiritual avenues, one affecting the other (emotionsanonymous.org).

There are a couple of misconceptions concerning the nature of the group's composition. First, as previously noted, EA does not posit that it is a replacement for psychotherapy if a person is engaging in said modality. However, it has been noted that it may be helpful to those who may be averse to traditional therapy. Next, EA has been described in several articles as a program for individuals with learning disabilities and the like, which is incorrect. EA does not specify a demographic population which it serves. The third tradition indicates all who wish to achieve better mental health are welcome (emotionsanonymous.org). The only thing that disappoints me about this fellowship is that there are not more meetings for people to take advantage of. At the clinic which I discovered EA, it was difficult finding a meeting which our patients could attend, despite it being in a large suburban area. However, this again may be a potential "silver lining" of the current state of society due to the Covid-19 pandemic. Let's hope so!

Conclusion

This concludes our exploration into some of the ways the modern psychotherapeutic techniques and philosophies coincide with the recovery program outlined in the 12-Steps of Alcoholics Anonymous. The 12-Step societies have evolved in several ways since its founding, incorporating new findings and discoveries in the fields of medicine and mental health. The mental health fraternity seems to have been more productive in incorporating the tenants of 12-Step recovery than the medical fraternity, in my opinion. Medicine seems to want to be the overriding authority in the fight against substance abuse. I do not know if this is the fault of the medical profession (pharmaceutical companies included) as a whole or if it is because insurance companies deem physical recovery more important than the recovery of body, mind and spirit. Physical recovery is a much faster process. A faster process means less time in treatment equaling less money paid out in the short term. If this is the reasoning behind medical recovery models, it is not a wonder that it seems like the problem is getting worse. Again, I alluded to my previous assertion that one cannot cure substance abuse by administering substances. This quick fix mentality coupled with an attitude of avoidance of pain and work may be the gestalt of today's society, but that is more likely the subject of another book or research project, so I digress. Though I must admit that seeing a television commercial for depression medication for one's pet is quite telling.

Although it can be argued that no system is perfect, I do hope without reserve that I am a part of the solution rather than a part of the problem. I have discussed some of the blemishes that I believe could be hindering treatment centers and clinics which raise these concerns within my mind, yet I remain hopeful. A particularly memorable personality that I met in early sobriety was embroiled in the topic of recovery success rates in AA's early years versus what seems a saturation of recovery centers trying to find a better way would often share his opinions on this matter. One night at a "newcomers meeting," a spot where numerous white vans from said recovery treatment centers would drop off their clients, this gentleman made a particular observation which struck me. What he said relates to the information presented in this volume and to the idea of keeping it simple; "They charge you thousands of dollars to come to their treatment centers to recover. Then they just throw you into a van and bring you here to AA and say get involved in this program."

This book presented several methods used in psychotherapy that not only overlap in the philosophical schools of thought that dominate today's clinical realm, but in 12-step societies to aid people in achieving satisfaction in their lives. These methods, when acted upon greatly assist the individual in attaining peace of mind, also known as serenity in their lives. When a person chooses to apply ideas such as mindfulness, delayed gratification, and the ability to respond to thoughts and emotions rather that react to them, their chances of engaging in relationships and situations which life presents in an effective and satisfying manner rises. Actions such as uncovering the nature of one's character defects with the intention of using these discoveries and insights to better navigate the interactions of daily life, rather than a justification of maladaptive behavior contributes in a similar fashion to a person's satisfaction with life. When a person chooses to be responsible for changing lifelong held perspectives and stories to narratives of empowerment rather than victimhood efficacy increases and life becomes more worthwhile. Instilling the understanding that it is not the responsibility of people, places, and things to not trigger the individual, but the individual's responsibility to cope with being trigger helps that person better live life on life's terms. The act of connecting with people, helping people and creating meaning in an otherwise mundane existence connects the individual to their spirit both internal and external, subsequently creating a more hopeful outlook to aid in carrying on. These are the goals, in my opinion of psychotherapy and is why I choose this profession. A personal hope is to aid in a synergistic phenomenon of affecting the world, making it a better place to exist one person at a time, one day at a time.

References

Adler, A (1997). Understanding Life; An Introduction to the Psychology of Alfred Adler.
One World Publications. Oxford. England. First Published as The Science of Living (1927).

Al-Anon Family Groups. "Suggested Al-Anon Preamble to the Twelve Steps". www.al-anon.org. Virginia Beach, Virginia: Al-Anon Family Group Headquarters, Inc. Retrieved 2014-01-18.

Alcoholics Anonymous (1939). Fourth Edition (2001). Alcoholics Anonymous World Services Inc. New York City. New York.

Ansbacher, HL; Ansbacher, RR (1956). The Individual Psychology of Alfred Adler. Harper and Row Publisher Inc. New York City. New York.

Corsenblum, B; Fischer, DG (May 1975). "Some correlates of Al-Anon group membership". Journal of Studies on Alcohol. 36 (5): 675–677.

Corsini, RJ; Wedding, D (2011). Current Psychotherapies. Brooks/Cole. Belmont. California.

National Institute on Alcohol Abuse and Alcoholism (1997), Project Match Hypothesis: Results and Causal Chain Analysis. U.S. Department of Health and Human Services. Rockville. Maryland.

Siegel, DJ (2012). The Developing Mind; How Relationships and the Brain Interact to Shape Who We Are. Mind Your Brain. The Guilford Press. New York City. New York.

Smith, MR; Patterson, GT (1992). Adult Children of Alcoholics Support Groups: A valuable adjunct in treating clients.

Van Wormer, K; Davis, DR (2008). Addiction Treatment; A Strengths Perspective. Brooks/Cole Belmont. California. USA.

Wallace, B. A. (2005). Balancing the mind. Snow Lion. Ithaca. New York.

Wilson, L (1995). "Lois's story". How Al-Anon Works for Families and Friends of Alcoholics. Virginia Beach, Virginia: Al-Anon Family Group Headquarters, Inc. pp. 136–137

Wright, KD; Scott, TB (September 1978). "The relationship of wives' treatment to the drinking status of alcoholics". Journal of Studies on Alcohol. 39 (9): 1577–1581.

www.adultchildren.org retrieved on 07/07/2020

www.emotionsanonymous.org retrieved on 07/07/2020

CPSIA information can be obtained
at www.ICGtesting.com
Printed in the USA
FSHW010507220421
80719FS